GOD'S LESSONS
AT THE 2010 CHILEAN MINE RESCUE

GOD'S LESSONS

AT THE 2010 CHILEAN MINE RESCUE

PETER WALTON
ILLUSTRATED BY JASON VELAZQUEZ

XULON PRESS ELITE

Xulon Press Elite
2301 Lucien Way #415
Maitland, FL 32751
407.339.4217
www.xulonpress.com

© 2021 by Peter Walton

All rights reserved solely by the author. The author guarantees all contents are original and do not infringe upon the legal rights of any other person or work. No part of this book may be reproduced in any form without the permission of the author. The views expressed in this book are not necessarily those of the publisher.

Unless otherwise indicated, Scripture quotations taken from the King James Version (KJV) – *public domain*.

Printed in the United States of America.

Paperback ISBN-13: 978-1-6628-1159-3
eBook ISBN-13: 978-1-6628-1160-9

DEDICATION

To everyone trying to break out of his or her cocoon to become a beautiful monarch butterfly soaring above and striving to live the purposeful life that God intended before you were even born.

ACKNOWLEDGEMENTS

To my wife, Haydee, for her passion for God.

INTRODUCTION

With God all things are possible.–Matt.19:26 (KJV).

We live in God's world, but we do not in the least know it as it is. We are very much in the position of a color-blind man in a beautiful flower garden. All around him are glorious colors, but he sees only blacks, whites, and grays. If we suppose him to be also devoid of the sense of smell, we shall see what a very small part of the glory of the garden exists for him. Yet it is all there, if he could but sense it.[1]

Outside we find the "marred image" showing limitation, sin, sickness, and inharmony…but underneath is the masterwork of the Great Artist, and our prayers act by clearing away the false accretions…so that the already existing truth and harmony may appear.[2]

It was God's hand, not coincidence, that the first thing the thirty-three miners did together after the collapse was to kneel in prayer to the Great I AM, to shield and protect them.

It was God's hand, not coincidence, that the Chilean miners exhibiting the national trait "to overcome adversity" survived seventeen

---

[1] Around the Year: A Book of Daily Readings by Emmet Fox. Harper One. Second Edition printed 1992. Emmet Fox lived on earth from 1886–1951. March 31, 90.

[2] Ibid., December 23, 357

days underground before contact was made with the surface. During this time, their drinking water was from the radiators of construction vehicles, and they had bare minimum food served once a day at noon, yet no one was physically sick during this time.

It was God's hand, not coincidence, that both the Chilean government and the drilling rescue teams from countries from multiple continents were at work twenty-four hours each day until contact was made on day seventeen.

It was God's hand, not coincidence, that just a few days before the day-seventeen breakthrough, a very rare rain in this, the driest desert on earth, caused a "desierto florido," a flowering desert, covering the landscape with flowers: fields of fuchsia, white star-shaped flowers, and yellow trumpets swaying in the breeze.

It was God's hand, not coincidence, that the drill broke through to the miners very early on a Sunday morning and that the note from the miners, saying that all thirty-three were well in the refuge, was found about 13:30 that afternoon by an unknown driller in a piece of rubber tubing with the note hidden inside.

It was God's hand, not coincidence, that both the high-tech professionals supporting the rescue efforts and the miners' families living on site could view the night sky and the many stars that God had created in the specific place on all of the earth where astronomers come from all over the world to view due to the sky's clearness in the desolation.

It was God's hand, not coincidence, that a small glass enclosed statue of Jesus's mother, Mary (Miriam), a gift from the Pope to honor the 2010 bicentennial of the creation of the nation of Chile, happened to be touring northern Chile and was brought on site.

It was God's hand, not coincidence, that after sixty-nine days the commitment to God by the thirty-three miners, the commitment to the rescue effort by people and companies from all over the world, and the commitment of the media to share the ongoing story with the world proved to the world God's power and miracles.

The goal of this book is best summarized by Emmet Fox:

The butterfly lived for what seemed to him a very long time as a humble caterpillar. Then one day the little caterpillar finds certain strange stirrings going on within himself. The old green leaf, for some reason, no longer seems sufficient. He becomes moody and discontented. He feels the need for a bigger, finer, and more interesting life. And so the wonderful thing happens; **the butterfly emerges beautiful, graceful, now endowed with wings, and instead of crawling about on a restricted leaf, he soars above the trees, above the forest itself—free, unrestricted, his own True Self.**[3]

> "Eye hath not seen, nor ear heard, neither have entered into the heart of man, the things which God hath prepared for them that love him."- 1 Cor. 2:9 (KJV).

---

[3] Ibid., April 15, 105

DAY 0, Thursday, August 5, 2010, 7:00 a.m.

Thirty-three miners are on a fifty-minute bus ride to their job at the San Jose mine in the Atacama Desert in northern Chile, one of the driest places on earth. Only once in a dozen years does rain fall on the mine. The mine was founded in 1889 to extract gold, copper, and iron.[4]

The night shift is done, and the miners are riding toward the surface in trucks. It will take forty minutes for the four-mile drive as the road snakes it way to the top from their work location 2,300 feet below.[5]

During their twelve-hour shift, the men have heard a distant wailing rumble as tons of rock have been falling in forgotten caverns inside the mountain. The men say to each other that the mine is "weeping" ("La mina esta llorando"). The wailing is not unusual, but the frequency is. It's as if they're listening to a distant growing storm.[6]

The men on the incoming shift exit their bus and are getting ready to ride on what's called "the ramp" to their work-site. On a standard day, with the temperature in the mine rarely less than ninety

---

[4] Deep Down Dark: The Untold Story of 33 Men In a Chilean Mine and the Miracle That Set Them Free by Hector Tobar published by Picador Paperback 2014, 3 and 15

[5] Ibid., 15

[6] Ibid., 15

degrees Fahrenheit, the men guzzle three quarts of fresh water to prevent dehydration.[7]

13:30: Two of the miners, Franklin Lobos and Jorge Galleguilos, are closest to the collapse. They hear a massive explosion, and the passageway around them begins to fill with dust. The roar is as if a massive skyscraper has crashed behind them.[8]

A block of diorite, later estimated to be as tall as a forty-five-story building, has broken off and is falling through the layers of the mine, causing a chain reaction as the mountain above it also collapses.[9]

The general manager of the entire mine is in his office when he hears constant rolling thunder. When he walks outside and looks at the mine entrance, he sees the largest cloud of billowing dust he's ever seen.[10]

---

[7] 33 Men: Inside the Miraculous Survival and Dramatic Rescue of the Chilean Miners by Jonathan Franklin published by Berkley Publishing Group 2011, 9

[8] Deep Down Dark: The Untold Story of 33 Men in a Chilean Mine, 27

[9] Ibid., 28

[10] Ibid., 28

After the initial shock, many of the men head up the road on vehicles. When the dust gets so thick that they can no longer see the road, a few of them exit the vehicles and proceed on foot. They sense something is blocking the road. They wait until the dust clears, then they see the size of the obstacle before them. It's a single piece of mountain which, afterwards, was estimated to be about 550 feet tall and 770,000 tons—twice the weight of the Empire State Building.[11]

The first few hours pass with the continual thunder of rock falling somewhere in the dark spaces beyond the weak light of their headlamps.[12]

Luis Urzua, the shift supervisor, is also a trained topographer and comes to the realization that in order for them to be rescued, a drilling that has never before been done will need to occur.[13]

Underground, Mario Sepulveda, a front-loader operator, becomes a leader. During the first hours of being trapped, Mario thinks often of his grandfather "who imparted the country ethic of hard work, respect and personal integrity." Mario had tried to mirror his life around the Chilean saying "to overcome adversity."[14]

The men take stock of their food and water inventory in the emergency cabinet in the small area of the mine known as "the refuge." They have a mere ten bottles of water. As a backup, they have several thousand liters of industrial water in the radiators of the many

---

[11] Ibid., 39
[12] Ibid., 56
[13] Ibid., 59
[14] Ibid., 60

construction vehicles, which they will be able to drink even though the water is tainted with small amounts of oil.[15]

For food, they have one can of salmon, one can of peaches, one can of peas, eighteen cans of tuna, eighteen liters of condensed milk, and ninety-three packages of cookies.[16]

All of the men are now in the refuge area. There should only be sixteen or seventeen, but there are miners working overtime or makeup days. Luis Urzua, counts to thirty-three. Mario Sepulveda and the rest of the men are struck by the number thirty-three, the age of Jesus Christ when He was crucified. Mario speaks: "Thirty-three. The age of Christ! (La edad de Cristo!) There are thirty-three of us. This has to mean something. There's something bigger for us waiting outside."[17]

22:00: They sit still, listening to the intermittent thunder of falling rock.[18]

Omar Reygadas goes to pray alone, sitting inside a front-loader. Tons of rock had fallen on top of them, yet none of the thirty-three miners have a scratch. To be alive against all odds speaks to Omar of the existence of a higher power with a plan for the miners.[19]

---

[15] Ibid., 66

[16] Ibid., 66

[17] Ibid., 67

[18] Ibid., 69

[19] Ibid., 71

DAY 1, Friday, August 6, 2010:

Pastor Jose Henriquez starts the day with a group prayer. Mario Sepulveda and a few others explore, looking for an escape. Mario climbs the designed escape ladder until it ends: it has never been completed.

God speaks to him: "I am with you." Reflecting on when they returned to the refuge, Mario said, "I came back and told them no one will die here-...-if you believe, hold God's hand and mine, and we will get out of here."[20]

---

[20] 33 Men: Inside the Miraculous Survival and Dramatic Rescue, 56-60

DAY 2, Saturday, August 7, 2010:

After a pessimistic statement by the Chilean Minister of Mining, a miner from another mountain who is a relative of one of the thirty-three, yells out: "David took on Goliath! And he used the weapons that he had!"[21]

At noon, Mario establishes the daily food pattern. One meal a day at this time. He lines up thirty-three plastic cups in rows and spoons one teaspoon of canned fish into each cup, then pours in some water to make a broth. Then each man gets two cookies. The total calories are less than 300.[22]

---

[21] *Deep Down Dark: The Untold Story of 33 Men in a Chilean Mine*, 82
[22] Ibid., 87

DAY 3, Sunday, August 8, 2010:

Pastor Henriquez continues to start the day with a group prayer.[23]

Some of the men put their ears to the stone walls, praying that they will hear the sound of drilling.[24]

Lyrics from a Simon and Garfunkel song come to mind:[25]

> "Hello darkness, my old friend,
> I've come to talk to you again
> Because a vision softly creeping
> Left its seeds while I was sleeping,
> And the vision that was planted in my brain
> Still remains
> Within the sound of silence."

Mario yells out: "I want to pray!" He falls to his knees, saying: "Those who want to pray, come and join me." He then asks Jose Henriquez to lead the men in prayer. From that moment on, Jose will be called "Pastor."[26]

Pastor asks the men to fall to their knees, then states: "Jesus Christ, our Lord, let us enter the sacred throne of Your grace. Consider this moment of difficulty of ours. We are sinners, and we need You. We want You to make us stronger and help us in this hour of

---

[23] 33 Men: Inside the Miraculous Survival and Dramatic Rescue, 64

[24] Deep Down Dark: The Untold Story of 33 Men in a Chilean Mine, 92

[25] The Sound of Silence lyrics © Universal Music Publishing Group, written by Paul Simon

[26] Deep Down Dark: The Untold Story of 33 Men in a Chilean Mine, 93

need. We need You to take charge of this situation-...-give us much strength (fuerza) and fortitude (fortaleza) to keep going-...-to get out of here-...-find a way to feed us."[27]

The men give individual testimonies and prayers, asking God to guide their rescuers to their passageway, while promising they will repent and begin their new lives as men of God.[28]

19:15: Seventy-eight hours after being trapped, they hear the sound of a drill spinning, grinding, and hammering against rock. For three hours the sound grows louder. By their calculation, the drill will make it through 100 meters a day, meaning it will take five or six more days to reach them.[29]

Above ground, an eight-member team of drillers makes a prayer circle to ask for God's help, and operator Nelson Flores places a rosary on the drill. Then they begin drilling.[30]

---

[27] Ibid., 94-95
[28] Ibid., 95
[29] Ibid., 101
[30] Ibid., 104

DAY 5, Tuesday, August 10, 2010:

Every day at noon, the men pray and have their one meal. With each day, more headlamps have gone dim; others are growing dimmer. This triggers much fear but also much prayer, as the men ask God to shield them from an unending darkness. One of the miners, Yanni Barros, feels there's something magical about the way the miners look in a weak light, standing or kneeling, listening to the Word of God.[31]

Edison Pena uses vehicle batteries to rig up a system of lighting to bring the men a constant beam of light, and Juan Illanes uses the batteries to design a system to charge the men's head-lamps.[32]

Outside in Camp Hope (Campamento Esperanza), where more than 1,000 family and friends of the miners have gathered, "prayer seems to be their only defense against the growing sense of hopelessness and finality."[33]

The area where they are drilling is expanding. At night, each drill's light seems insignificant against the black of the total desert darkness.[34]

---

[31] Ibid., 96

[32] 33 Men: Inside the Miraculous Survival and Dramatic Rescue, 64-65

[33] Deep Down Dark: The Untold Story of 33 Men in a Chilean Mine, 115

[34] Ibid., 118

DAY 6 and on, starting Wednesday, August 11, 2010:

They continue with their daily noon prayer and meal.

Pastor Jose Henriquez sometimes tells the parable of Jonah being swallowed by a whale due to his disobedience, consigned to the belly of hell in the depths of the ocean. He would state the following from the Bible: "I went down to the bottoms of the mountains. The earth with her bars was about me forever."

(Jonah 1:6 KJV). After Jonah promised God that he would sacrifice unto God with thanksgiving, the whale spits him out.[35]

Trapped inside these stone walls, the pastor's messages make the men feel as though they're living a Bible parable.[36]

They're becoming physically weaker. On August 15th, their 11th day underground, Victor Segovia writes in his journal that many of the men are losing hope. This continues, exacerbated by the sounds of drilling being very close until it misses them. Then the drilling sounds get further and further away.[37]

On August 17th, the drilling sounds are quite close, then the men realize the drilling is below them and growing quieter and quieter. This is the eighth miss. On the 19th, they're close to starvation, down to one cookie every other day and their version of water. Then, a drill misses for the ninth time.[38]

---

[35] Ibid., 130
[36] Ibid., 131
[37] Ibid., 137
[38] Ibid., 138

The miners' metabolisms are slowing down, and they're experiencing severe weight loss. They're beginning to have visions and unusually long, vivid, real-life dreams similar to what people doing long fasts experience. The men's dreams take them to places of memory and desire, mind dramas from their personal histories with casts made up of their loved ones.[39]

Juan Illanes has been working to remember a song he sang as a teenager in a church choir. It takes him four days to recall all sixteen lines of the four stanzas. He goes off alone to a place in the mine where no one can hear him and sings the entire song, which ends with "Only in Him did I find happiness" ("Solo en El encontre la falicidad")."[40]

---

[39] Ibid., 142

[40] Ibid., 146

DAY 16, Saturday, August 21, 2010:

They have one meal every two days—half a cookie and a single slice of peach, about the size of a thumb divided thirty-three ways. The men each treat their sliver, the size of a fingernail, like a communal wafer.[41]

One of the smallest of the men, Claudio Yanezis, is no longer getting up. Mario orders him to rise. Claudio tries to rise to his feet with buckling knees and bent legs. To one of the miners, it is like watching a newborn foal trying to walk.[42]

---

[41] Ibid., 149

[42] Ibid., 152

DAY 17, Sunday, August 22, 2010:

Within Camp Hope, the boyfriend of one of the miner's daughters plays his guitar and sings. He and many of the family members have had their spirits and faith lifted seeing the desierto florido, the flowering desert. A rare rainstorm passes through the desert to briefly moisten the land. The result: a super bloom of flowers—purple fuchsia, white star-shaped flowers, and yellow trumpets.[43]

One stanza of the song he writes:[44]

> "The rocks of the mountain fall apart,
> The miners will soon come out,
> The chimney has collapsed,
> But your Father will soon bring you out."

05:00: Mario Sepulveda, in the deepest sleep he can remember, is having a dream of his grandparents. His grandmother has brought him a basket filled with food. Then his grandfather tells him, "Get up from there, hombre. You are not going to die here. (Vos no vas a morir aqui)." Mario wakes up to the grinding and pounding sound of a drill that's becoming impossibly loud.[45]

The men hear another drill getting closer, targeting their 33-foot-long, 540-square-foot section of the mine. The drill breaks through! Due to a rescue class one of the miners had taken at another mine, the miners are prepared, so Richard Villarroel continuously pounds on the length of the pipe that the drill is attached

---

[43] Ibid., 155

[44] Ibid., 156

[45] Ibid., 157-158

to with a 2-foot wrench, attempting to prove to the world they are still alive.[46]

All thirty-three men have gathered around the pipe and the drill bit object that have entered their dark world with the promise of being raised up into the light. Jose Henriquez, transformed into a shirtless, starving prophet, states that God exists ("Dios existe").[47]

06:00: Above-ground, the recognition of the noises from the hammering of the drill pipe below have confirmed that some miners are alive.[48]

Monica Avalos, the sister of Florencio Avalos, walks around Camp Hope amongst the embraces and celebrations. She can see the people's breaths visible in the early morning light as they give multitudes of thanks to God in their prayers.[49]

---

[46] Ibid., 153, 159-160
[47] Ibid., 160
[48] Ibid., 164
[49] Ibid., 167

The drill team is slowly removing the 115 400-pound steel tubes from the shaft one at a time, a process that will take until early afternoon. The last section is pulled up. The drill team washes away the muck, which reveals red paint. A note from Mario Gomez survived the journey and is read: "May God Illuminate You."[50]

A piece of rubber tubing is found with something hidden inside. The Minister of Mining reads the message: "Estamosm Bien En El Refugio. Los 33. (WE ARE WELL IN THE REFUGE. THE 33)." The drilling teams erupt. Some fall to their knees in thanks and prayer. Some of the drillers cry "the way men do when their mothers die, or when their sons are born."[51]

All the other drills have stopped. Some drillers run to Camp Hope to let the family and friends know the news! -The cheering spreads across the mountain, with the cries of the drillers the loudest.[52]

President Sebastian Pinera arrives. He shows the note to the cameras, which sets off celebrations across Chile. People all over the country run from their televisions to the streets and plazas. Throughout Chile and Bolivia, the peals of church bells ring through the Sunday air. The Bolivian Carlos Mamani is the only miner not from Chile. Day0 was his first time working at the mine![53]

---

[50] Ibid., 168-169

[51] Ibid., 170

[52] Ibid., 170

[53] Ibid., 171

DAY 18, Monday, August 23, 2010:

Pedro Gallo is a local businessman who runs a communication company. He has been on site since August 6th. An official from Codelco, the government-run National Copper Corporation of Chile, asked him to make a phone line so there could be an audio connection between the surface and the miners. In forty-five minutes, he puts together a telephone receiver and transmitter from a piece of plastic molding, a few thousand feet of discarded wire, and some old telephone components.[54]

14:30: Thirty-three-plus hours after the drill first broke through, miner Edison Pena has a direct connection to the surface, talking with the Minister of Mining, Laurence Golborne. When Minister Golborne acknowledges that he can hear Edison Pena, two dozen men surrounding him burst into cheers. The mining minister then relays to the miners that the entire country is participating in the rescue with their prayers and celebrations.[55]

Down below, the thirty-three men cheer, humbled by the information that the entire country has been thinking about them, praying for them, and working to rescue them.

The miners choose Luis Urzua, the shift supervisor, to be on the phone. His first question is to ask if Raul Villegas, the thirty-fourth man in the mine at the time of the collapse, made it to the top during his drive to safety. When the surface responds yes, the

---

[54] Ibid., 176

[55] Ibid., 176-177

miners celebrate again. The first phone call with the surface ends with the miners singing the Chilean national anthem.[56]

As much as the men want to spend an entire day gorging on food, the first nutrition sent down to them is thirty-three clear bottles with a few ounces of glucose gel. NASA has brought packets that U.S. astronauts use while in space.[57]

The first letters from their family members on the surface at Camp Hope are sent down.[58]

---

[56] Ibid., 178
[57] Ibid., 178
[58] Ibid., 184

DAY 19, Tuesday, August 24, 2010:

President Pinera is talking to the miners from La Moneda, the presidential palace in Santiago, letting them know he's reached out to the world for the technological help needed to extract the miners. He doesn't share the specifics with the miners, but he had learned from the tragic event of the sinking of the USSR nuclear submarine *Kursk*. The *Kursk* sank on August 12, 2000, with a crew of 118. It may have been an impossible task, but only a Communist government would deny the offers for help that they received from other countries. Rather than try, they did nothing as the Morse code signals from the crew asking for help grew fainter and fainter until silent.[59]

He does share with them an idea of how long it's going to take to build the infrastructure needed to remove them.[60]

Many of the men have just regained enough strength to rise to their feet after the connection to the surface. The news of the estimate as to how long before they can be rescued has returned grim and exhausted expressions to their sooty faces. The mine is still trembling and thundering around them. Any moment, a new collapse could destroy the life-giving shafts that link them to the surface.[61]

Jose Henriquez admonishes the men to remember that they should thank the Lord for the miracles that have already unfolded before them.[62]

---

[59] Ibid., 184
[60] Ibid., 184
[61] Ibid., 185
[62] Ibid., 185

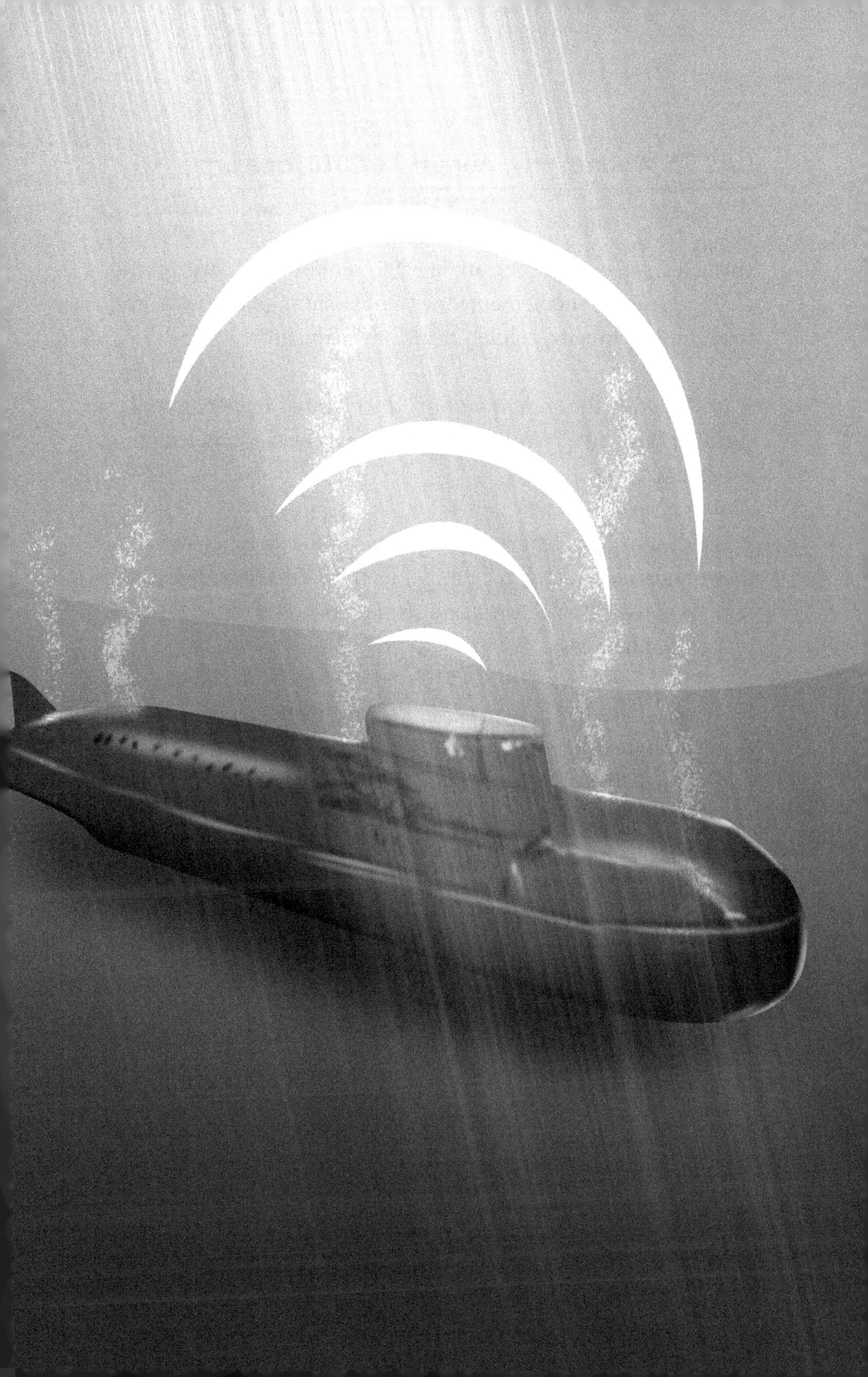

DAY 20, Wednesday, August 25, 2010, and on:

The first few days, the men are fed 500 calories a day, largely with an energy drink supplemented with potassium, phosphates, and thiamine. Eventually, regular meals start to be provided.[63]

A poster with the pictures of all thirty-three men is popular throughout Chile: "We Are Waiting for Them" (Los Estames Esperando).[64]

When the throng of reporters and producers file their news reports, they're often serenaded by family members on site with cries of faith, promises of salvations, and reminders not to forget the thirty-fourth miner, Jesus Christ.[65]

The families have set up a special area with Chilean flags where family members and/or friends go to light candles late each day, just before night.[66]

---

[63] Ibid., 187

[64] 33 Men: Inside the Miraculous Survival and Dramatic Rescue, in the photo section after page 148

[65] Ibid., 160

[66] Ibid., 161

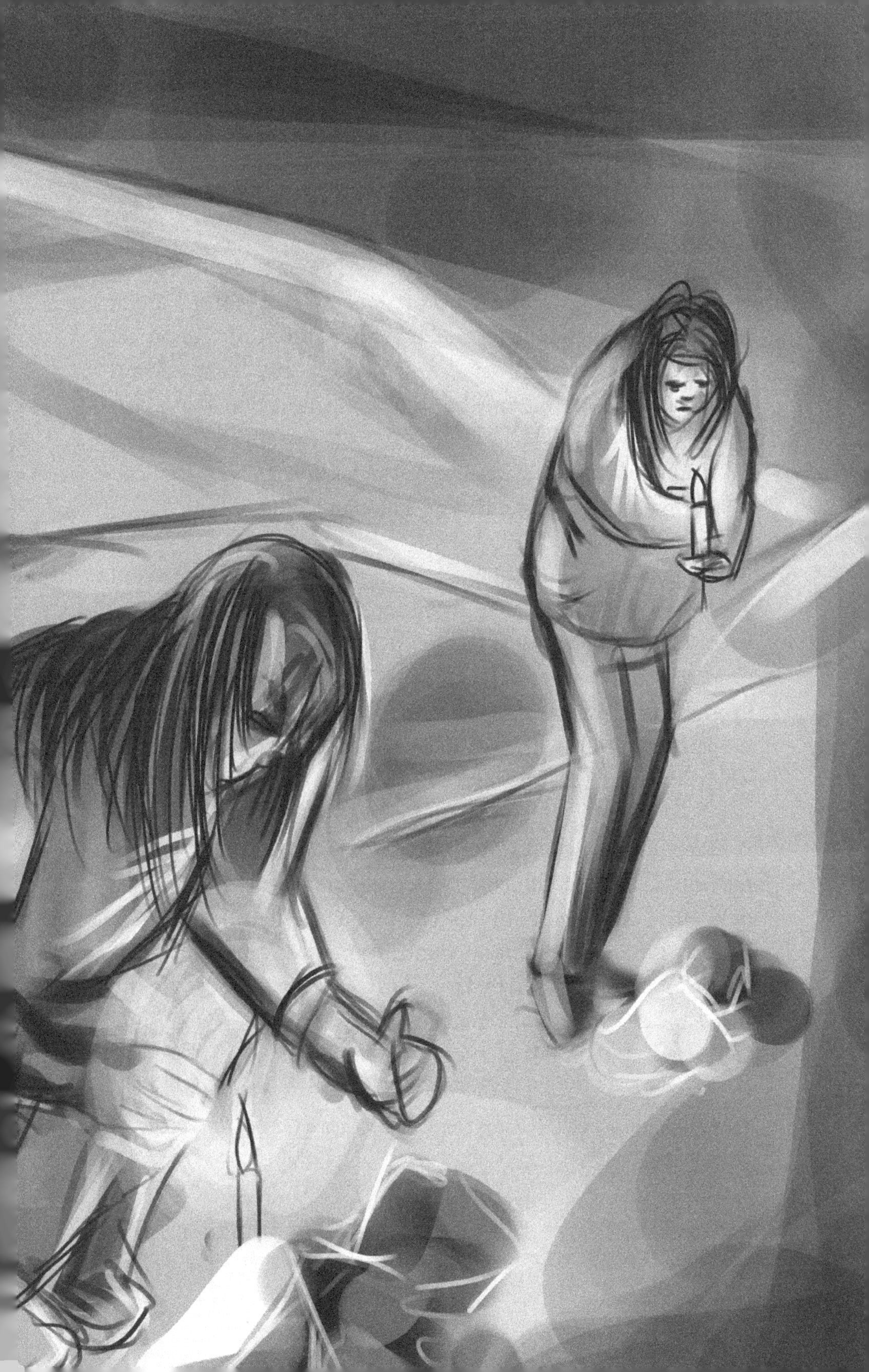

DAY 29, Friday, September 3, 2010:

The miners create a video, which is edited down to eight minutes to be shown on Chilean television. One excerpt is from Victor Zamora, who thanks the rescuers while the rest of the miners applaud and chant, "Chi-chi-chi, le-le-le." Next, Osman Araya praises and thanks God, and the miners sing the national anthem.[67]

In Victor's journal, he states that he knows how an animal in captivity feels—always dependent on a human hand for food.[68]

Drilling experts and drilling technology from around the world are headed for the mine from multiple cities in multiple countries: Johannesburg, South Africa; Berlin, Pennsylvania; Denver, Colorado; and Calgary, Canada; as well as from a U.S. Army base in Afghanistan. Center Rock, Inc., in Pennsylvania, sends one of its' clustered drills with UPS offering to deliver it free of charge, where it will arrive September 11th.[69]

Brandon Fisher from Center Rock arrives on site to share how his company drilled down 240-feet and created a 30-inch-wide hole, then raised nine miners one by one to the surface at the Quecreek mine in Somerset County, Pennsylvania. The men had been trapped for over three days. The last man was brought to the surface at 2:45 a.m. on the morning of Sunday, July 28, 2002. One of the men, Tom Foy, is now working for Center Rock.[70]

---

[67] Deep Down Dark: The Untold Story of 33 Men in a Chilean Mine, 190

[68] Ibid., 198

[69] Ibid., 199-200

[70] Trapped: How the World Rescued 33 Miners From 2,000 Feet Blow the Chilean Desert by Marc Aaronson published by Atheneum Books 2011, 75

Three NASA officials arrive. At night, they take in the spectacle of the night sky over the Atacama Desert, where for decades, astronomers have come to view the stars without manmade distractions.[71]

Down below, the men can not view the Milky Way, as they spend hours in the stillness and in the heat that comes from the center of the earth.[72]

In a letter to him, Louis Urzua's wife, Carmen Berrios, gives details on the complex of machines and vehicles that has been used in the recovery effort, the numbers of workers, the huge floodlights, the newly created roads, and the shipping containers.[73]

Edison Pena starts running solitary in the mine. Since the contact with the surface, he promised God he would show his devotion and gratitude by running. He's seen the light of faith in the mine as a blue light.[74]

---

[71] Deep Down Dark: The Untold Story of 33 Men in a Chilean Mine, 214
[72] Ibid., 215
[73] Ibid., 221
[74] Ibid., 226-227

DAY 37, Saturday, September 11, 2010:

The daily prayer sessions, which originally included all thirty-three men, are now down to six or seven. Mario Sepulveda goes to a place in the mine by himself to read Bible verses. He practices giving a sermon to a congregation, as he sees himself travelling the world to both praise God and to thank the Chilean workingman once he gets to the surface.[75]

He believes that the devil has attached himself to the letters the miners have received from above and has created thoughts of money and fame to separate the men and initiate envy, greed, and misunderstanding.[76]

He prays that God will make the men united as before and confesses that he's afraid of evil and needs God to strengthen and protect himself and the rest of the men.[77]

Just as Mario is praying, he hears a tremendous crash—the sound of a huge stone slab that has broken off and landed ten feet away. He recoils in shock and fear, and at the same instant, he feels the presence of someone just behind him, a hot breath on the back of his neck. He turns around and swings his lamp on a pool of water, seeing a pair of half-crazed, startled eyes looking back at him. They are his own eyes and his own face covered with fear.[78]

---

[75] Ibid., 233-234
[76] Ibid., 234
[77] Ibid., 234, 235
[78] Ibid., 235

"Diablo! You'll never take me. I'll never be your son!" he proclaims. Then he runs three-quarters of a mile uphill back to the rest of the miners.[79]

Ariel Ticona's daughter, Esperanza, is born. His sister films the birth in the hospital, and he's shown an edited video. It's the first time in human history that someone trapped below the earth has witnessed the birth of his child.[80]

---

[79] Ibid., 235

[80] Ibid, 238

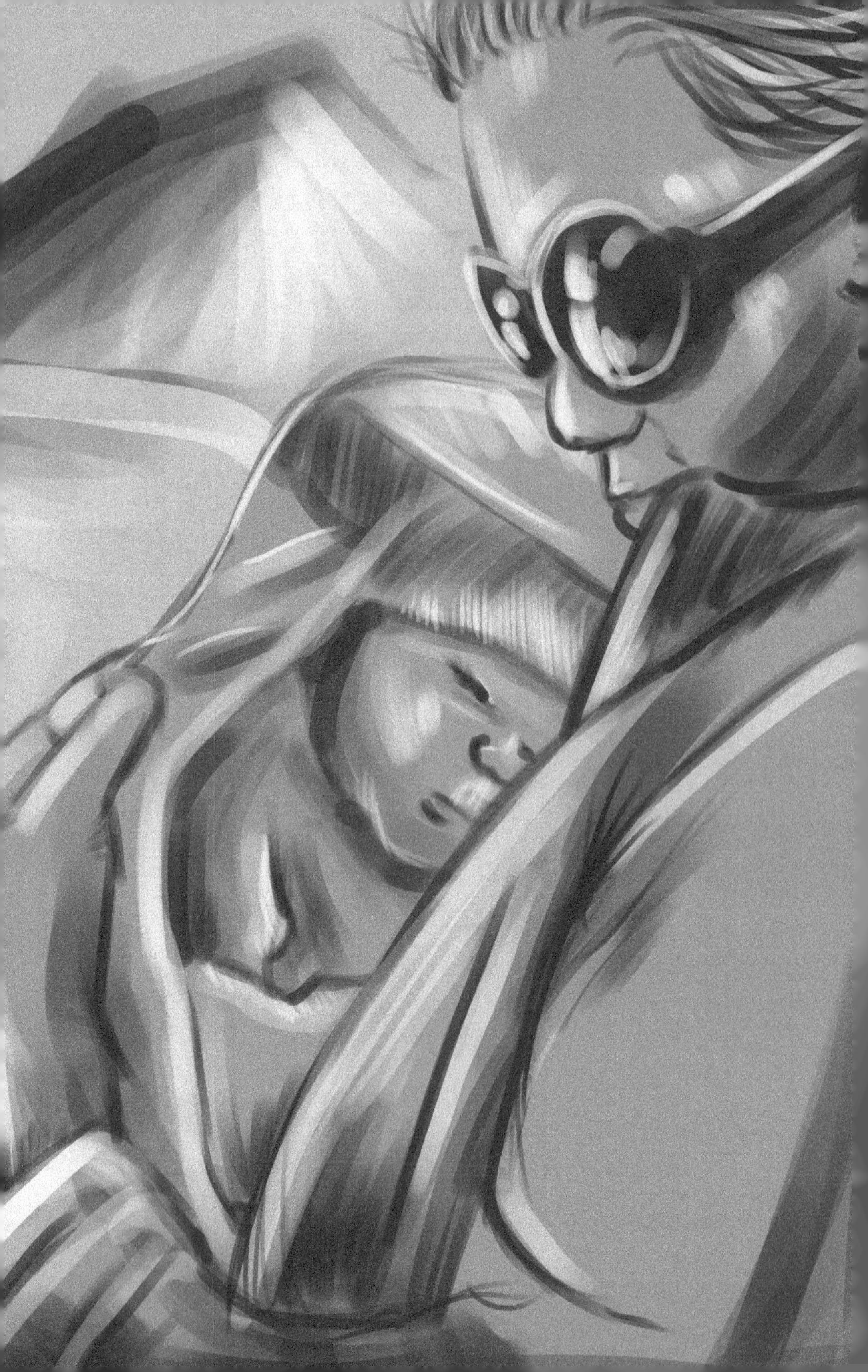

The Chilean navy announces the specifications for the escape capsule they're building. They've named it the Phoenix (Fenix) after the bird that rises from the ashes in Greek mythology.[81]

---

[81] Ibid., 239

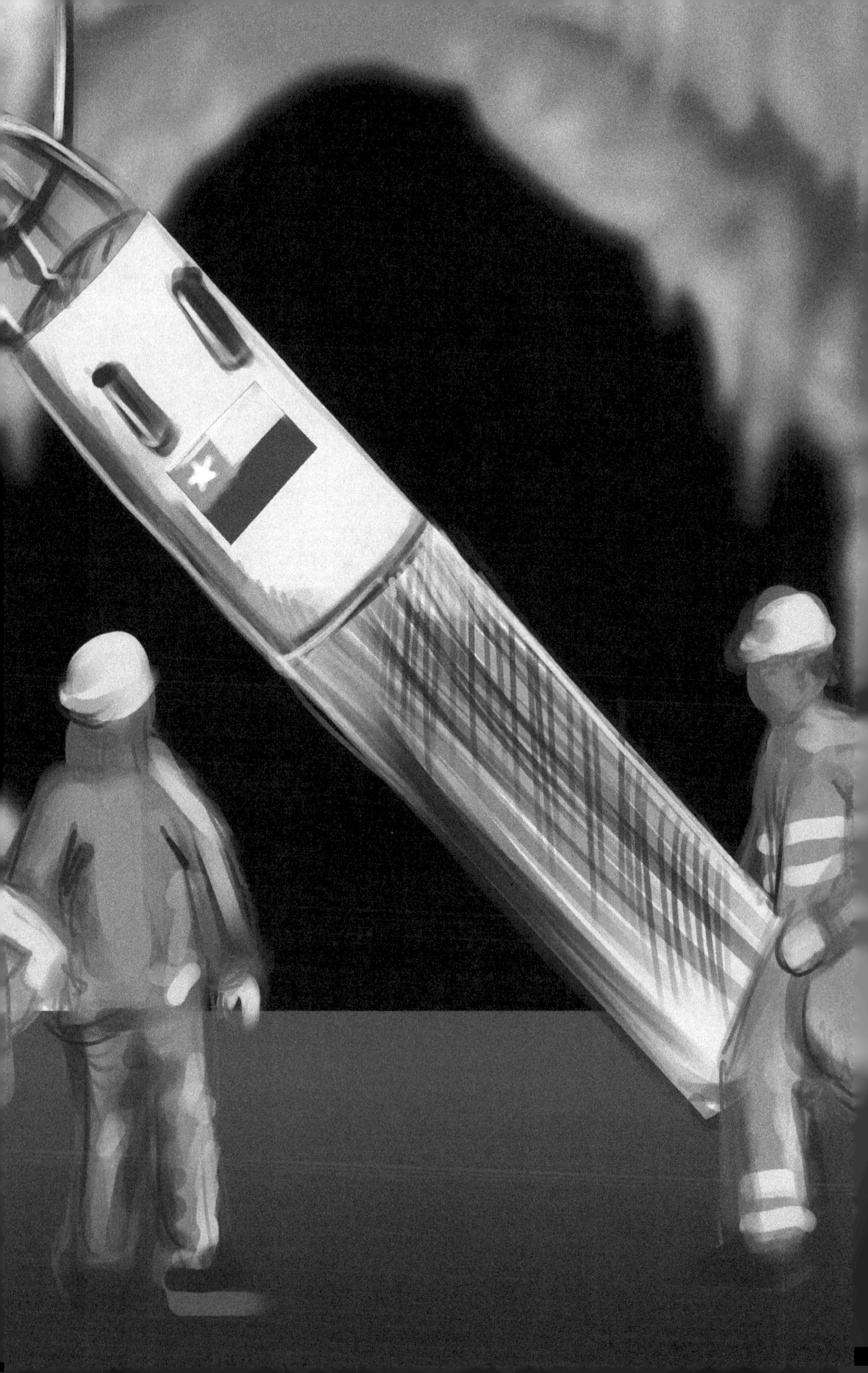

DAY 39, Monday, September 13, 2010:

22:00: The Virgin Mary arrives at the site. Pope Benedict XVI has commissioned a wooden sculpture to be created and given to Chile to commemorate the country's bicentennial. She's in a glass case and has been touring northern Chile. Many women from the family camp come over and pray, holding candles. In the flickering yellow light, the faces of the women have a glow kinder than the gray flood lamps over the camp.[82]

---

[82] Ibid., 231,232

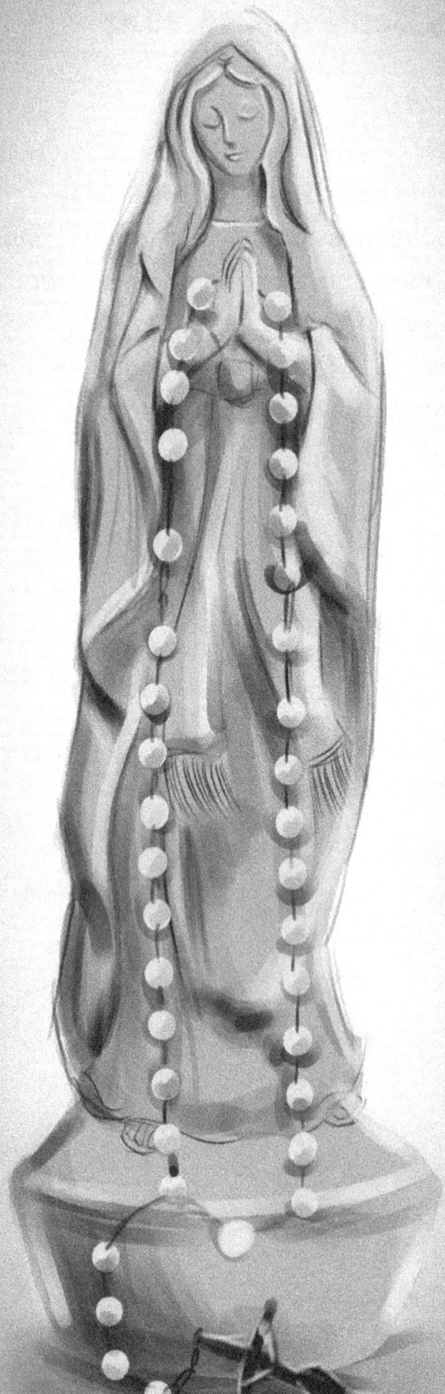

DAY 43, Friday, September 17, 2010:

The second stage of the rescue plan progresses when a drill breaks through. There is now a seventeen-inch-wide hole linking the men to the surface. The next stage is to expand this to twenty-eight inches.[83]

---

[83] Ibid., 241

DAY 46, Monday, September 20, 2010:

On the surface, four American drillers and their Chilean colleagues begin drilling to widen the seventeen-inch hole.[84]

---

[84] Ibid., 244

DAY 65, Saturday, October 10, 2010:

From above, the rescue workers inform the miners that the drill is less than 33 feet from breaking through. The men huddle 160 feet from where they have prayed the drill would break through.[85]

Jeff Hart and the T130 crew are less than a foot away from breaking through when the drill emits a loud pop. Surprisingly, the drill keeps going with the same pressure, and they never find out what has caused the pop.[86]

Underground, the roar of the drill chewing and pounding the rock is painfully loud to the men, even though they're wearing earplugs and earphones. At 8:00 a.m., the drill breaks through.[87]

As the nub of the drill breaks through the roof, a massive cloud of dust fills the caverns. Many of the men have flashbacks of the first cave-in. But this time, the dust storm is a glorious sign of freedom. The miners celebrate.[88]

Minister Golborne has stated that the crews would set off a siren when the drill breaks through. At 8:02 a.m., the wail of the siren travels across the mountain. In Camp Esperanza, family members celebrate then call out, "To the flags," rushing to the collection of thirty-two Chilean flags and one Bolivian flag to continue their celebration.[89]

---

[85] 33 Men: Inside the Miraculous Survival and Dramatic Rescue, 222-223

[86] Deep Down Dark: The Untold Story of 33 Men in a Chilean Mine, 254

[87] 33 Men: Inside the Miraculous Survival and Dramatic Rescue, 224

[88] Ibid., 224

[89] Deep Down Dark: The Untold Story of 33 Men in a Chilean Mine, 254

The men have one last planned explosion at San Jose. They plant dynamite at the bottom of the Plan B shaft then detonate it so that the capsule will be able to reach all the way to the ground for their individual entry.[90]

The twenty-eight-inch-wide rescue shaft delivers a welcome breeze of fresh air to the tunnel. The men marvel at the pleasure of the cool air, not knowing that the same rescue hole so close to delivering them to safety is also a potential death trap. The cooler air from above is causing the walls of the mountain to contract, thus destabilizing the mine.[91]

---

[90] Ibid., 254

[91] 33 Men: Inside the Miraculous Survival and Dramatic Rescue, 228

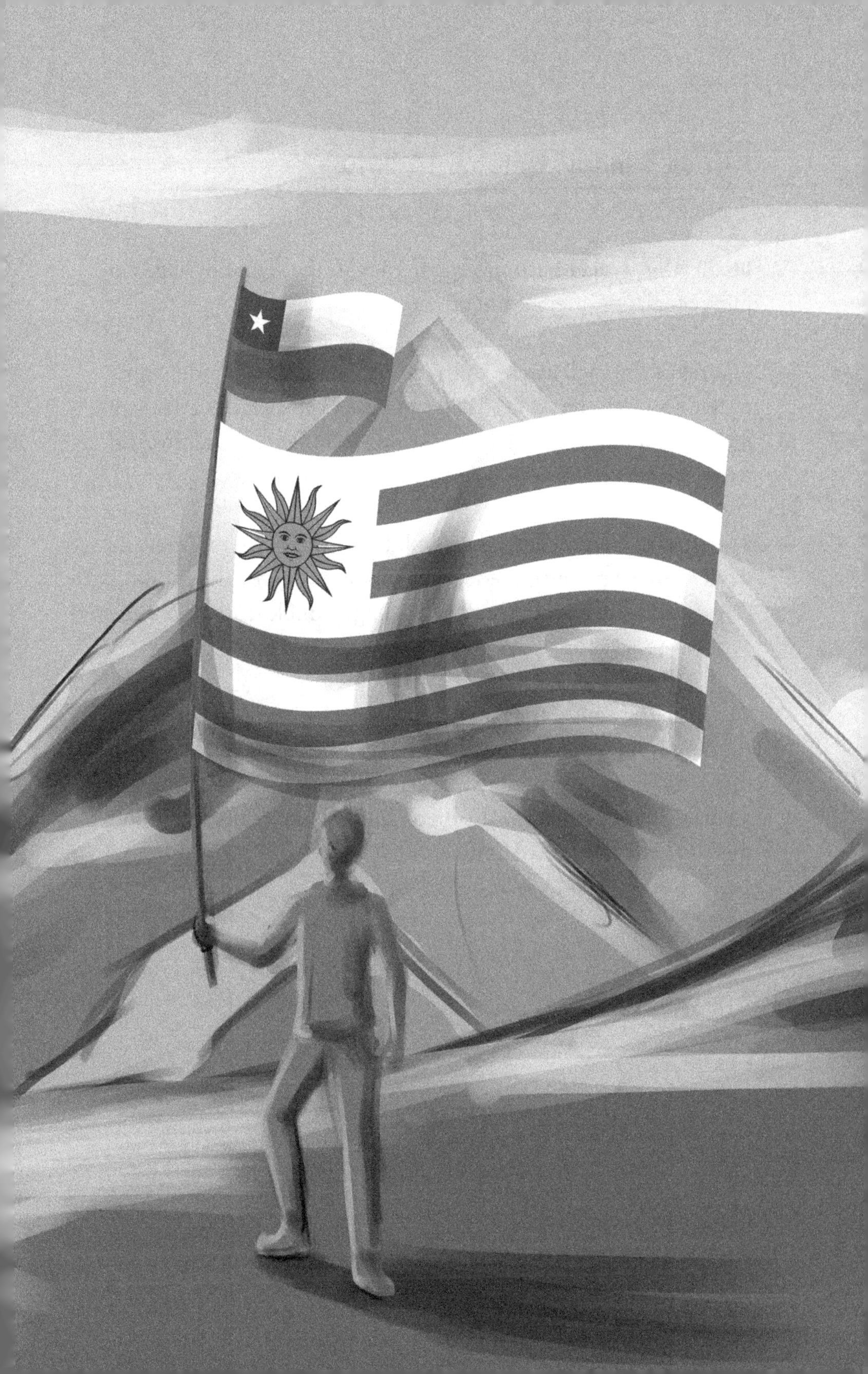

DAY 66, Sunday, October 10, 2010:

06:00: This danger becomes apparent with the sound of huge rippling roars, one after another.[92]

Several of the men awake to the sound of distant thunder transmitted through the stone. They can hear explosions like a storm inside the mountain—a series of strong thunderclaps coming just a few seconds apart. This will continue for four hours.[93]

Some of the men believe the rumbling is the devil and that the devil is angry because the men are about to leave. The thunderclaps inside the mountain end with a huge rumble from below like a massive rockslide.[94]

To Omar Reygadas, the cacophony of rocks being let loose is a warning from God that they have to keep believing in Him, keep thanking Him for giving them life, and keep praying that they will all make it to the surface. The mountain was exploding to remind them to keep their word.[95]

---

[92] Ibid., 228
[93] Deep Down Dark: The Untold Story of 33 Men in a Chilean Mine, 255
[94] Ibid., 255-256
[95] 33 Men: Inside the Miraculous Survival and Dramatic Rescue, 229

DAY 68, Tuesday, October 12, 2010:

The mountain rebels again—another avalanche from below. The roof of the mine is groaning. The sound is like the rumbling of an avalanche, and the crash of rocks coming down is a reminder that the miners' salvation is still not guaranteed.[96]

Victor's last diary entry reads: "The earth is giving birth to its 33 children after having them inside her for two months and eight days."[97]

23:08: Manuel Gonzalez is the first rescuer sent to the miners. He's a miner at the El Teniente mine, about fifty miles south of Santiago, where he's a member of their rescue team.[98]

23:34: Manuel arrives below where the miners are gathered. His job will be to supervise the loading of the thirty-three men into the capsule. There are a total of six rescuers being sent to aid in the miners' departure.[99] The camera visuals of Manuel's arrival down below look like they were taken from a remote-controlled vehicle from a distant planet.[100]

---

[96] Ibid., 251

[97] Deep Down Dark: The Untold Story of 33 Men in a Chilean Mine, 259

[98] Ibid., 245

[99] Ibid., 245

[100] 33 Men: Inside the Miraculous Survival and Dramatic Rescue, 256

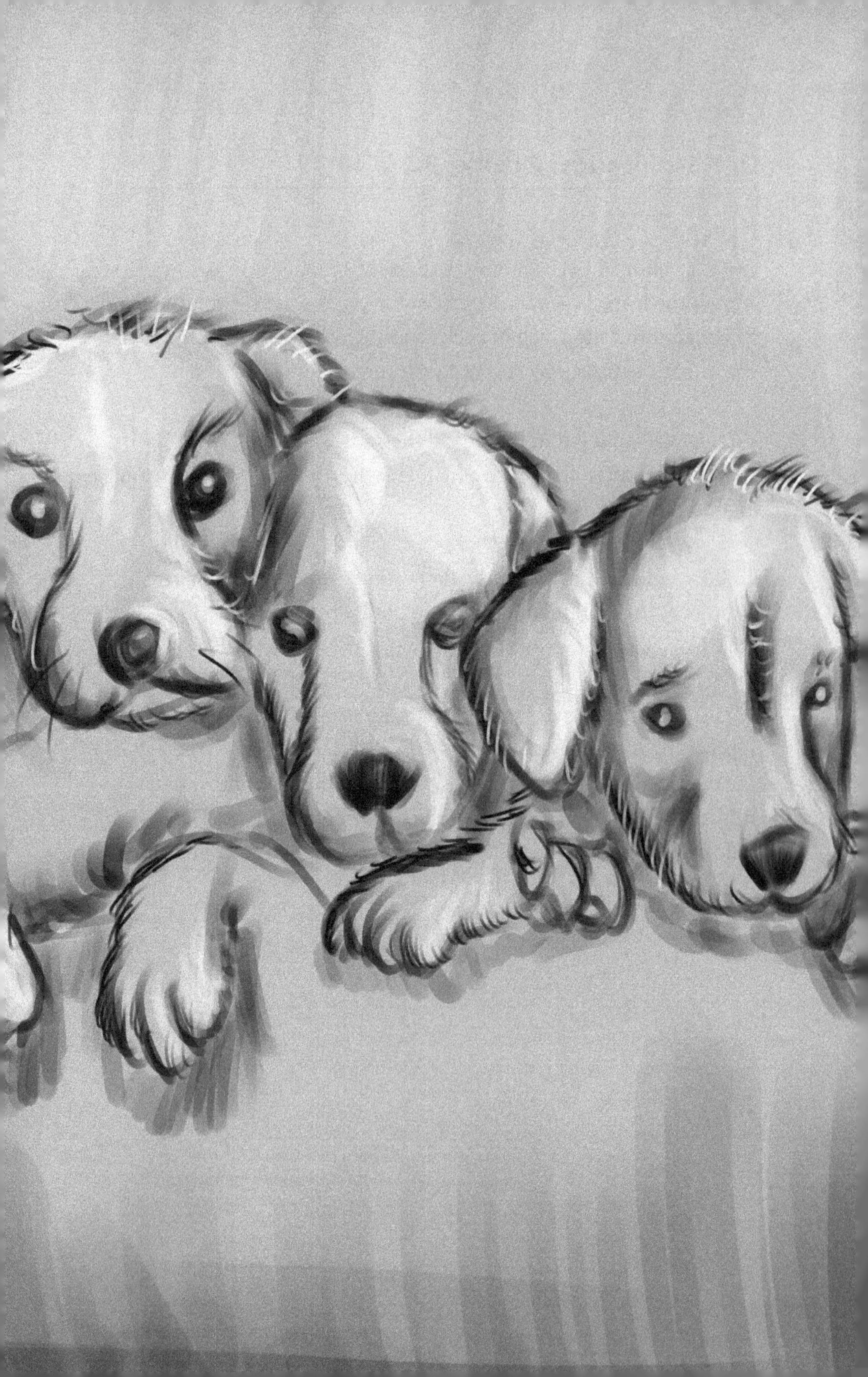

DAY 69, Wednesday, October 13, 2010:

Florencio Avalos will enter the capsule and be the first of the miners to make it to the surface. Just before he enters, the men bow their heads to say a final prayer. Sixty-nine days earlier, they fell to their knees and asked God to lift them out of this place. Now, they ask God to protect Florencio in this first journey of deliverance.[101]

The men "will rise up through a 2,100-foot birth canal carved into the mother mountain."[102]

Florencio leaves for the surface, strapped inside the Phoenix, just before midnight on Tuesday, October 12th. His thirty-minute ride will bring him to the surface in the first minutes of Wednesday, October 13th, provided everything works as planned. His arrival will be seen on live television by 1.2 billion people, one-fourth of the world's population. He arrives on the surface.[103]

---

[101] Deep Down Dark: The Untold Story of 33 Men in a Chilean Mine, 261

[102] Ibid., 264

[103] Ibid., 264

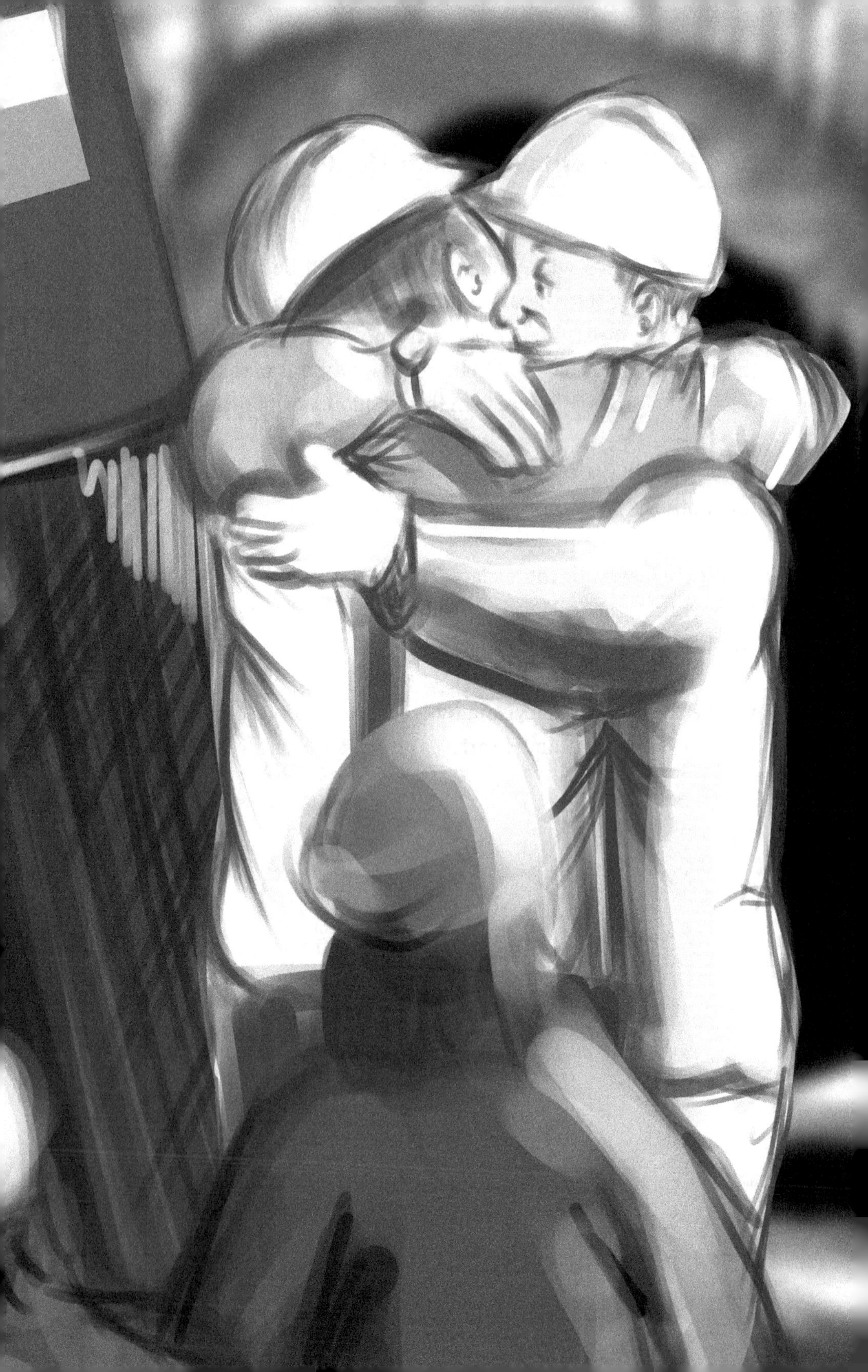

"Ministers, hardhat rescue workers, doctors, and journalists all wept openly at the beauty of the scene."[104]

Mario Sepulveda is the second miner who rides the Phoenix to the surface. He and Florencio are taken to the field hospital on site at the mountain. He's interviewed on television: "I was with God and the Devil, and they fought over me. God won. I took the best hand, the hand of God, and never did I doubt that God would get me out of the mine. I always knew."[105]

---

[104] 33 Men: Inside the Miraculous Survival and Dramatic Rescue, 260
[105] Ibid., 263

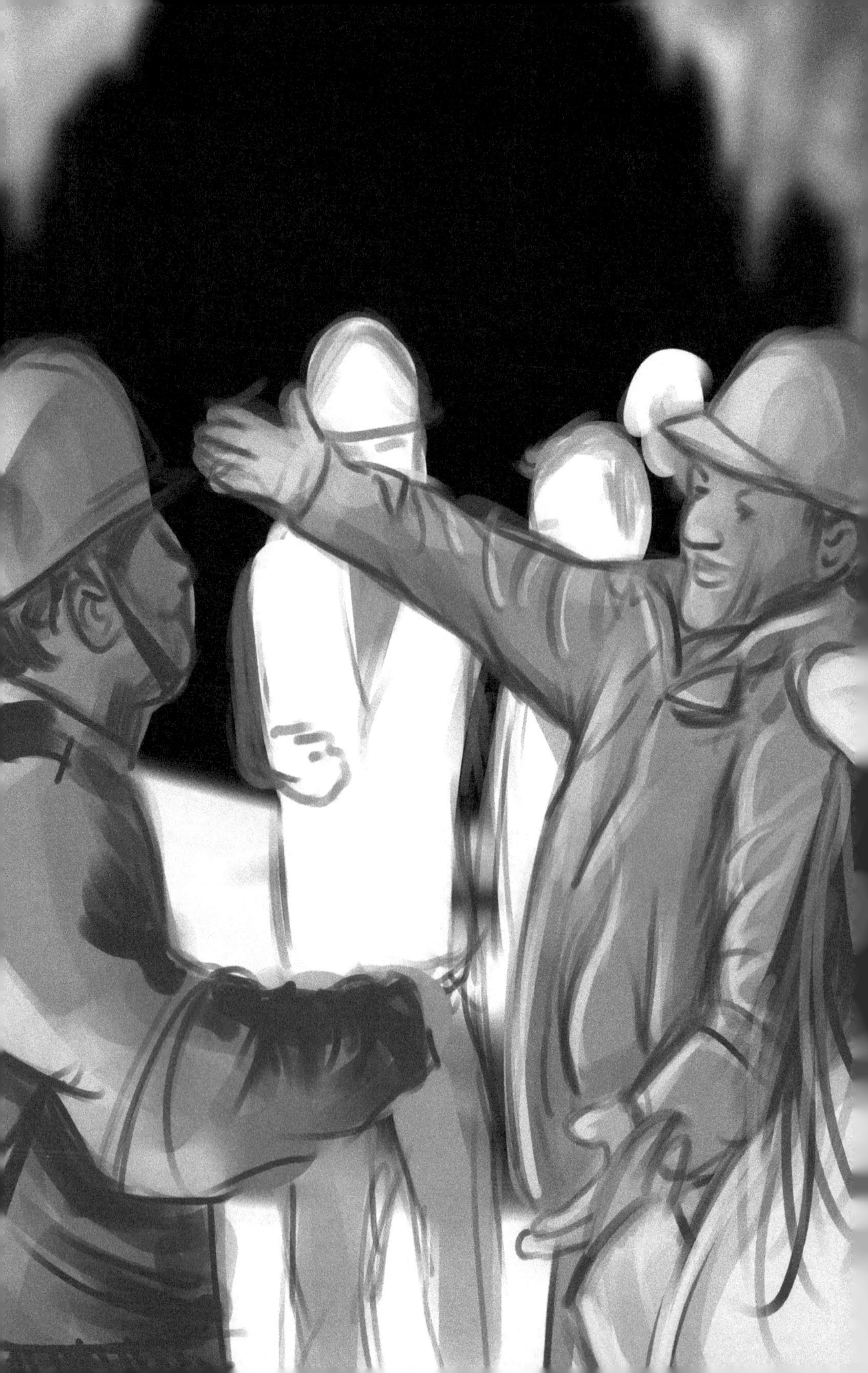

When Samuel Avalos and seven other miners are taken in a helicopter to a hospital in Santiago, they stare in disbelief at the tents, buildings, roads, and parking lots, amazed at the transformation of the barren mountainside. The men ask the pilot to make an extra loop over the rescue site. They're beginning to understand the scale of Operation San Lorenzo.[106]

At **1:30 p.m.,** as the capsule comes down to pick up miner number seventeen, Omar Reygadas, a sharp crack echoes through the tunnel, followed by the crash of boulders and the rumble of an avalanche. The rescue is no longer being shown live on television. Operation San Lorenzo is blind.[107]

The head of the telecommunications post, Pedro Gallo, comes up with an alternative and asks miner Pedro Cortes to go to the safety refuge 1,000-feet below the miners' location to disconnect a cable and rewire the fiber-optic cable to the main camera filming the rescue. Cortes is hesitant, as the refuge is close to the most recent avalanche, but he perseveres, actually making two perilous solo journeys, the last one taking nearly one hour.[108]

After miner number two, Mario Sepulveda, arrives, a miner is brought back into the light thirty-one more times. The last miner, Louis Urzua, the shift supervisor, says the following to President Pinera: "As the jefe (the boss), I hand over the shift to you."[109]

---

[106] Ibid., 277

[107] Ibid., 265

[108] Ibid., 265-269

[109] Deep Down Dark: The Untold Story of 33 Men in a Chilean Mine, 270

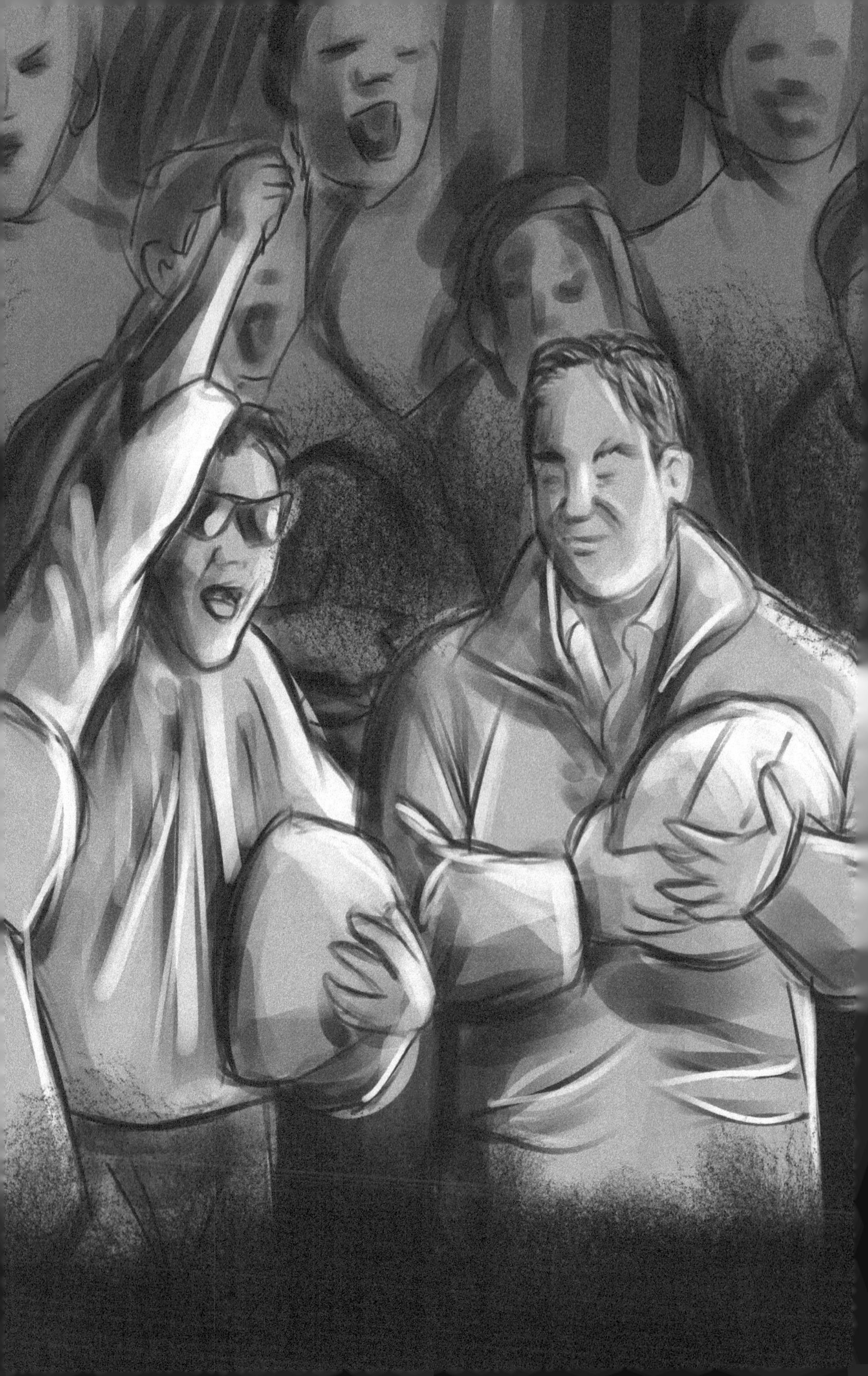

There were five other rescue workers who were sent down along with Manuel Gonzalez: two from Codelco, two navy marines, and one from GOPE—police special operations. After the miners are all up, the six rescue workers come up, with Manuel being the last one. After Manuel arrives, President Pinera says, "Today Chile is not the same country it was sixty-nine days ago."[110]

---

[110] Ibid., 271

EPILOGUE

Individual experts on underseas, underground, and outer space and companies from Australia, Austria, Canada, Japan, South Korea, and the United States all contributed to the rescue.[111]

The miners benefited from the latest technology and information, fiber-optic cables, cell phone projectors, NASA's studies, nutrition information, and biometric belts. The most important reason the men came home safe was their trust in God and one another during the first seventeen days, when they had no contact with anyone above.[112]

Faith and technology literally moved a mountain. The miners, families, rescue workers, and world media worked together toward a common goal.[113]

It is estimated that for every trapped miner, thirty to fifty people worked full time on the rescue effort.[114]

Behind the scenes, or better stated, underneath the scenes, were the modern tools that made the whole operation possible. This

---

[111] Trapped: How the World Rescued 33 Miners From 2,000 Feet Below the Chilean Desert by Marc Aaronson published by Atheneum Books 2011, 92

[112] Ibid., 92

[113] 33 Men: Inside the Miraculous Survival and Dramatic Rescue, 296

[114] Ibid., 297

included GPS units that allowed the massive drills to find a tiny underground target, miles of fiber-optic cable, and wireless transmitters that relayed the miners' pulse and blood pressure to a physician's laptop.[115]

A few weeks after their October 13th rescue, Pastor Jose Henriquez spoke at an evangelical church in Santiago with several of the miners present: "I could see before me thirty-two men humbled before God. Now, I thank the Lord for this opportunity to testify to the great power of God. What God did in that place is undeniable. And let no one rob God of His glory. That's why we're here."[116]

---

[115] Ibid., 6

[116] Deep Down Dark: The Untold Story of 33 Men in a Chilean Mine, 287

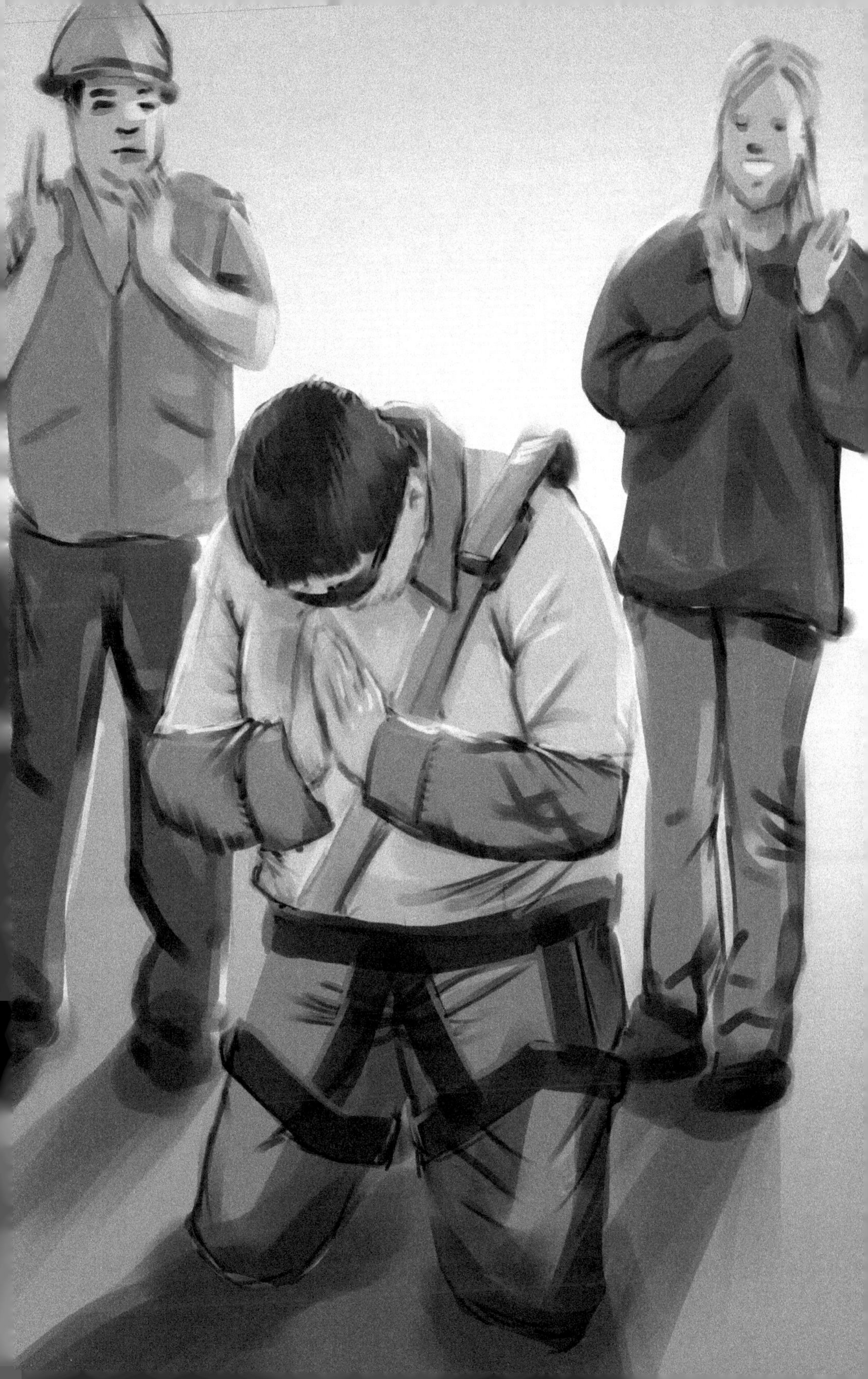

PREQUEL TO THE CHILE MINE RESCUE

Quecreek Mine accident, Somerset, Pennsylvania, from Wednesday, July 24, 2002, through Sunday, July 28, 2002.

BEFORE

The first commercial coal mining in the thirteen colonies was in Richmond, Virginia, in 1750. In Somerset County, Pennsylvania, coal mining started in the early 1800s. From 1850 to 1950, coal was the United States' most important fuel, as coal was "used to melt glass, heat forges, kiln lime and cement, and process wood pulp. Coal-powered railroads moved the country's goods and coal-steam engines drove factory machines."[117]

Definition: kiln: a furnace or an oven for burning, baking, or drying, especially one for calcining lime or firing pottery.[118]

After coal's heyday from the 1920s through the 1930s, the coal industry fell on hard times in the 1950s and 1960s, when nuclear power and oil seemed to be the energy sources of the future. Coal

---

[117] All Nine Alive Pittsburgh Post-Gazette 2002 Triumph Books Chicago, 20

[118] www.dictionary.com

was considered a relic of the Industrial Age, one that was soon to be replaced.[119]

This changed in the 1970s with two events. First was the embargo of oil-producing Arab nations, starting in October 1973, against countries who supported Israel during the Yom Kippur war. This embargo caused the price of oil to increase over 300 percent, leading to increased gas prices in the U.S. as well as a gas shortage (Wikipedia: 1973 Oil Crisis). Second was the Three Mile Island 'meltdown' that occurred at a nuclear power plant on March 28, 1979, in Middletown, Pennsylvania. Although there were no injuries or deaths at the plant or in the local community, public opinion turned against using nuclear energy. (Wikipedia: Three Mile Island accident).

As a result, in the 1970s, coal once again became America's fuel source of choice. In the 1980s, however, the role of coal in the United States changed again due to environmental regulations as the U.S. steel industry, a large user of coal, shut down numerous plants. The power industry switched to natural gas.[120]

At the Quecreek Mine, each shift produces between 1,000 to 1,500 hundred tons of coal with a monthly target of 55,000 tons.[121]

In the last eighty years, coal output in the United States has doubled, rising from 564 million tons in 1923 to over 1,100 million

---

[119] Our Story: 77 Hours That Tested Our Friendship and Our Faith. By the Quecreek Miners as told to Jeff Goodell published by Hyperion New York 2002, 6

[120] Ibid., 6

[121] Nine For Nine: The Pennsylvania Mine Rescue by Andrew Morton 2002 published by Michael O'Mara Books Limited London, 31

in 2001.[122] The bulk of this comes from the big strip mines in Kentucky, Wyoming, and West Virginia.[123]

There are two separate nine-man crews drilling at Quecreek on July 24th. In each crew, "the miner cuts the coal, the shuttle car driver hauls it away, the bolters secure the roof, the scoop driver cleans up the mess. When it's going right, it's a symphony of heavy machinery-….-there is even a kind of elegance and beauty in it. In the darkness and noise, you feel deeply connected to your buddies, your machinery, and the earth itself."[124]

"Mining is more than just a job; it is a way of life, one that involves a communal lifestyle whose values and operations hark back to a different era, a world incomprehensible to the soft-handed sons and daughters of the computer era."[125]

Randy Fogle is the foreman of one of the two nine-man crews. The men were working in an area that, according to their maps, was 300-feet from the old Saxman mine, which had opened in 1923 and yielded four million tons of coal before closing forty years later.[126]

The map was incorrect. What was about to be unleashed into the Quecreek mine was what was estimated to be between sixty million and over one hundred million gallons of water—a "subterranean reservoir" that had built up naturally in the Saxman mine since its' closure in 1963.[127]

---

[122] Ibid., 45
[123] Our Story: 77 Hours, 6
[124] Ibid., 12-13
[125] Nine For Nine, 45
[126] Our Story: 77 Hours, 17
[127] All Nine Alive, 25

Wednesday, July 24, 2002:
20:44:

Mark Popernak is working the miner machine, cutting into the coal face, when the old Saxman mine is breached. Thousands of gallons of a yellowish liquid, barely recognizable as water, burst over the top of his five-ton machine, turning his twenty-foot-wide section into a furious rapidly rising torrent. Popernak has been operating the continuous miner by remote control and is tucked behind a coal pillar when the first torrent explodes into the mine. The pillar saves him from being washed away. With the bright lights of the miner extinguished, he only has the flickering beam of his cap lamp to light the scene. He has been separated from his coworkers, and the terrifying surge of water is racing past and over him. He yells at Dennis Hall to leave right away.[128]

20:45: In the noise and confusion, foreman Randy Fogle requests that Dennis Hall call the other crew of nine-miners, who are working lower in another section of the mine. Ron Schad has received the phone call from Hall and alerts the rest of this crew. He and Larry Summerville are riding a golf-cart two minutes ahead of the other seven men, trying to find a mine exit.

They realize that their only hope is to find the intake door that leads to the three-foot-high ventilation shaft. As they enter the air shaft, they realized that if the doors or the block walls don't keep the water out, they are done for. The water pouring on either side of the four-inch-thick walls sounds like thunder, and the pressure of the flood is forcing jets of water through every little gap in the walls.[129]

---

[128] Nine For Nine, 53-54

[129] Ibid., 60-61

Just before it blows open, Ron and Larry crawl past the first man-door. Ron looks back then, and though he can see nothing, he hears gushing water sounding like a combination of Niagara Falls and thunder. When he hears the "boom" of the second door bursting, he fears the rest of the crew has drowned and that in a few moments, he too will be swallowed up in the swirling, filthy flood. He recalls, "I asked God to grab a hold of me and help me out. 'Get me out,' I prayed."[130]

The other men of the second crew have no choice but to crawl into the three-foot-high intake tunnel with water pouring through the gaps between the blocks and the sound of a furious, pounding torrent in the darkness.[131]

They have to dive into the icy water, into the swirling maelstrom. Barry Carlson is sucked under and later stated that at the time he was thinking of his brother's death in a mine many years ago. Dave Petree sees his fellow miner go under and crawls back and anchors himself to a cable with one hand, then grabs Barry with the other hand. Dave's son Ryan then helps him pull Barry back to where they were.[132]

Again, they hear the frightening "boom" sound as another man-door blows open somewhere behind them. Joe Kostyk's prayer at the time is, "Just give us a few more steps, God, just give us a few more steps, and we'll make it."[133]

---

[130] Ibid., 64-65
[131] Ibid., 61
[132] Ibid., 62-63
[133] Ibid., 63

Once all nine men of the second crew make it to ground level, their concern is for the other crew still in the mine. All nine will remain on site until Sunday's rescue. This is the origin of the phrase "Nine for Nine."

Between 23:30 and midnight, Larry Summerville goes back to look for the other crew in a two-man golf cart. He goes down too far and is forced to retreat as water comes roaring in from another section. When he shines his cap light at the approaching water, he glimpses a miner's raincoat and a pair of rubber gloves floating on the current. "For a moment he thought he was looking at a corpse. They proved to be only articles long abandoned in the mine, but it was an unnerving moment."[134]

Eight of the miners are trapped together, and one, Mark Popernak, is by himself, isolated by a raging current. As the water rises in the forty-two-inch passage, the eight men unknowingly take the same approach that the first group of miners took going into the air shaft. By now the rising water level has resulted in them going from having a four-inch space at the top of the passage to being completely underwater. They have to swim back twenty feet to the crosscut, and the only air they can find is in a slim, narrow space at the roof.[135]

Popernak waits several hours for the water to slow down, but it doesn't. He thinks he is the only one left in the mine and decides he will try to swing across on the roof bolts to cross the raging river. He makes it to the second bolt but feels the next one will be his last because he can't hold on anymore. He turns his cap light

---

[134] Ibid., 75

[135] Miracle at Quecreek Mine by Bill Arnold published by Encourage Publishing 2017, 26

off and closes his eyes to say a prayer for his family. He then sees John Phillippi motioning for him to get back. He is seconds from being swept away to drown and end up somewhere in an unknown cavern of the mine.[136]

The miners decide they will try to rescue Popernak and get him back on their side of the water. "If they were going to die, they would die together." They tear a wall down and drive one of the scoops out into the current as far as it is safe. Then Popernak makes the jump of his life into the back of the bucket. They go together to the number-four entry and huddle beside the heat of a roof bolting machine.[137]

Just before midnight:

Bill Arnold is the owner of the Dormel Farm and has eighty-plus cows. His dog's barking wakes him, and after arming himself with his Colt 45 handgun and a flashlight, he goes to investigate. He finds two men, both of whom he knows. They are surveyors from CMR Engineering: Sean Isgran and Bob Long. They inform him that there has been an accident at the Quecreek Mine and they need to drill a hole on his land to provide air to trapped miners. They are using GPS to determine how to reach coordinates they had been given thanks to Quecreek Mine manager and owner Dave Rebuck's detailed maps of the location of the highest point in the mine where they believe the miners would go. Rebuck's company is Black Wolf Coal. Another surveyor, Dave Zwick, uses a manual method and comes up six inches from the GPS spot. They mark the spot for the air hole three inches in between the two spots.[138]

---

[136] Ibid., 27

[137] Ibid., 27

[138] Ibid., 24

Thursday, July 25, 2002:
02:50:

Lou Bartels of Bartels Drilling begins to drill the six-inch air shaft and drills 240-feet to break through in the twenty-foot target dead center at **04:35**. At that time there are six people above ground working on getting air to the men. After some confusion, they finally realize that someone below has banged on the pipe they lowered.[139]

"We found out later that the six-inch drill had broken through just in time. The miners were ready to suffocate. There was no oxygen left in the mine, and they were breathing very hard. One guy said they could count the number of breaths they had left on both hands-....-If anything had been out of place—if the surveyors had needed to start their process over, if the drilling had not gone smoothly, if the equipment had not been readily available—those miners would have died. But God had it all worked out."[140]

Below ground, the miners try frantically to build a wall to stop the advancing water. They stack cinder blocks and try to make them watertight, adding mud and grit into any gaps. They can hear the drilling above them as their air is rapidly running out. "As the sound of the drill grew louder and louder, their hearts beat faster and faster as they gasped for air. They were down to their last few breaths."[141]

"Then suddenly the drill punched through-....-With the drill bit came the compressed-air pipe which for the moment landed in a

---

[139] Ibid., 29-33

[140] Ibid., 33-34

[141] Nine For Nine, 83

pool of water. One of the men grabbed it and let the good air wash over them, drawing it deep into their oxygen-starved lungs."[142]

The Sipesville Fire Department provides airbags they use when extracting people injured in car accidents to seal the drill in the six-inch hole so that no air will escape. The air being sent down is bubbling up through the water to the highest point in the mine, creating an air pocket exactly where the miners are. But the water continues to rise.[143]

Once the miners recover with their fill of oxygen, they follow the instructions inside each miners' hat and first hit the pipe three times, which signifies men in danger. They then hit the pipe nine times to state that all nine miners are alive.[144] Above them, rescue workers shut down every piece of machinery, apart from the compressor, to listen for sounds from below. Suddenly, tapping comes back through the steel. Above ground, they hear the sequences of three taps, then nine taps. "That was our sign that our prayers had been answered," said Louis Bartels.[145]

11:45:

"By noon Thursday they had completed five cinder block walls, but it was all to no avail. The water overtook them as they worked on the sixth. They had to retreat to the highest ground, about 300 feet from the airshaft near entry no. 1. There they would wait for what seemed to be the inevitable as the water rose closer and closer. The

---

[142] Ibid., 83-84
[143] Miracle at Quecreek Mine, 34
[144] Our Story: 77 Hours, 72
[145] Nine For Nine, 84

water lapped seventy feet away." Randy Fogle, their leader, gives it to them straight: in another hour, they will all be dead.[146]

Blaine Mayhugh takes out a piece of cardboard and writes a note to his wife and two sons to tell them he loves them. The other miners write similar notes, and the notes are then put in a plastic bucket and lashed to a bolter machine so they will be found.[147] Moe (Mark) Popernak recalls: "My note was short. I made it short because I wanted everybody to have time to write their note and the water was coming really fast."[148]

Tom Foy (Tucker) suggests that the men loop a forty-foot-long steel cable through their belts, which they will also tie to the bolter so that their bodies will be recovered. Six of the men do so, two say they will at the last moment, and one refuses to join.[149]

"Their preparations complete, there was nothing to do but wait. At this point the water was thirty feet below them-….-a big pool of flat black water inching slowly toward them-….-And the terrible irony was, Randy and his crew were all passionate fishermen."[150]

The men talk about drowning. Flathead (John Phillippi): "I wished we'd just run out of air and pass out because I didn't know how I would do this. Are you going to put your head tight to the roof and try to keep as much air in your lungs as you can? Or are you just going to go under?" Moe talks about "drowning with dignity."[151]

---

[146] All Nine Alive, 46

[147] Ibid., 46

[148] Our Story: 77 Hours, 93

[149] Ibid., 95

[150] Ibid., 95

[151] Ibid., 96-97

In the darkness, the men recite the Lord's Prayer, waiting for death:[152]

> "Our father which art in heaven
> Hallowed be thy name
> Thy kingdom come, Thy will be done in earth,
> As it is in heaven
> Give us this day our daily bread
> And forgive us our trespasses as we forgive those who trespass against us
> And lead us not into temptation, but deliver us from evil:
> For thine is the kingdom, and the power, and the glory, for ever and ever. Amen."
>
> -Matt. 6: 9-13 (KJV).

"As the water rose—it was now about twenty feet away—Randy and his crew were confronted by a final dilemma. Were they going to stay there at the bolter and let the water rise over them, or would they scramble to the highest ground in the mine—a small area a few hundred feet away, in the back of entry one? It was only a few feet higher, but it would buy them a few more breaths of air." They move up.[153]

---

[152] Nine For Nine, 97

[153] Our Story: 77 Hours, 99

Peter Walton | 71

Above ground:

Water from the mine is now four inches from the top of the sixteen-foot-high garage door at the mine entrance. Bob Long and Sean Isgran have once again used their GPS software to map six drill sites for water removal. Calls go out to drilling companies throughout the state and beyond for drills that can reach 300 feet below. Companies involved in well drilling rush to the site. They know they have to lower the water level in the mine ASAP.[154]

In addition, they need a superdrill that can bore a thirty-inch diameter hole to the men so they can ride a twenty-two-inch rescue capsule to the top. The rescue capsule itself is being rushed from its' location in West Virginia. A father and son team, Gene and Duane Yost, have such a bit weighing in at 1500 pounds. They live in Greene County, south of Pittsburgh, and bring the bit with them. The forty-six-foot-high rig needed for this is at another site, also in West Virginia. The West Virginia and Pennsylvania state police coordinate to escort the five-truck convoy containing the rig at top speed, and it arrives on site at 14:30. It then takes five hours to set up, with drilling beginning at 19:30.[155]

During the day, family members gather at the century-old Sipesville firehall, supported by clergy from the eight different churches the nine trapped miners attend. The hall contains an artist's rendition of three firefighters hoisting a U.S. flag on September 11th at Ground Zero in New York City.

---

[154] Nine For Nine, 98-99

[155] Ibid., 99-100

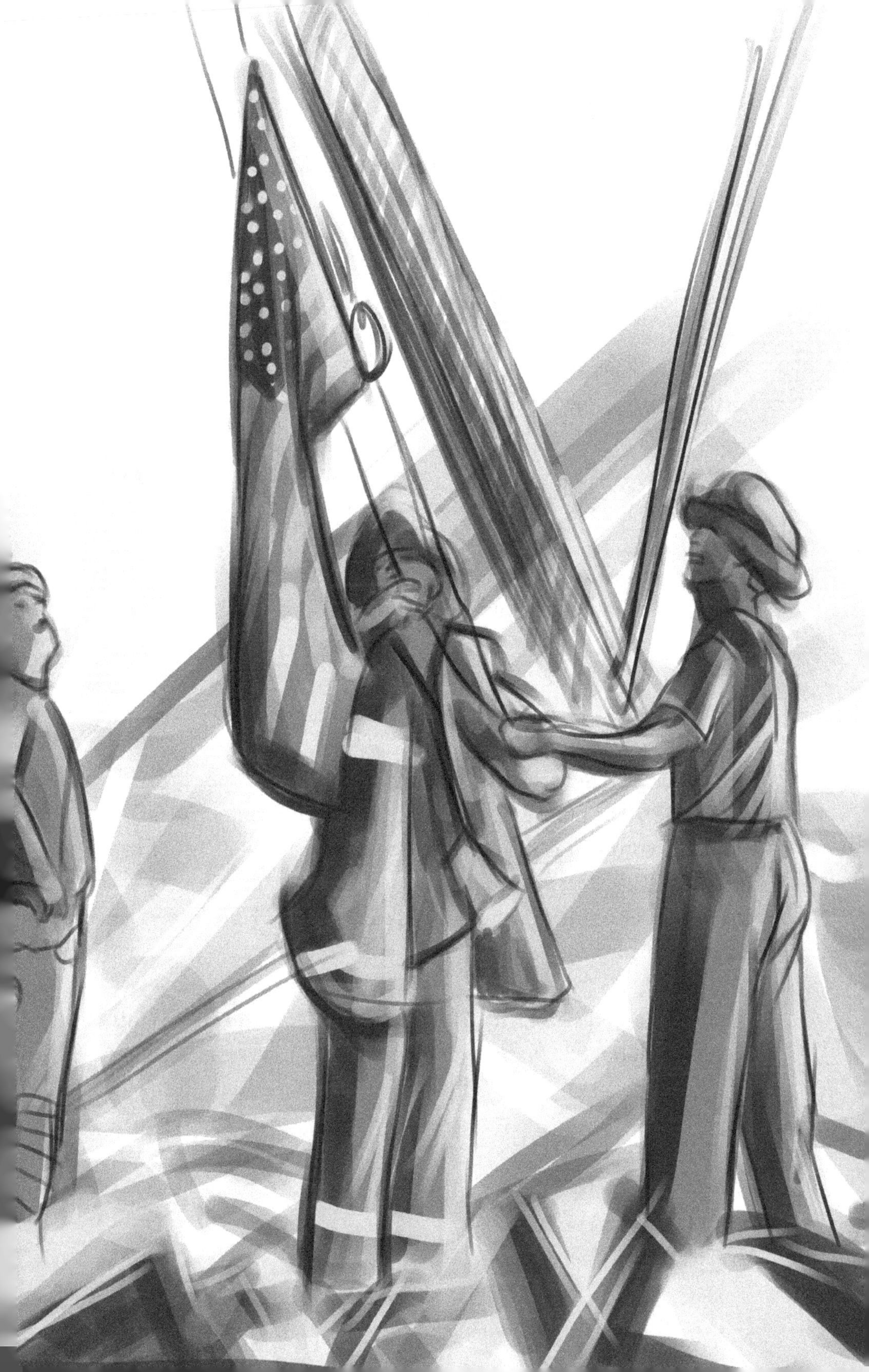

Down below, the men are in "a small rectangular area about twenty feet wide by seventy feet deep at the top of entry one-....-But this was it: the absolute highest point in this section of the mine. From here, there was no retreat." They huddle in ventilation canvas to keep warm and use canvas to put up a wall against the water.[156]

They sit in darkness for long periods of time to save the batteries on their lamps. The men can hear the drill coming toward them.[157]

Above ground, two huge diesel water pumps, plus four smaller ones, are removing 36,000 gallons of water a minute.[158]

Equally important, a prayer chain wraps itself around all the churches in Somerset County.[159]

Friday, July 26, 2002:
01:50:

The miners can hear that the drilling of the RD-50 super drill has stopped. Driller Duane Yost calls the command center: "Control, we've got a problem." The bit on the super drill at drilling site 1 has broken.[160] This is eerily similar to Apollo 13 astronaut Jack Swigert's words to the command center on April 14, 1970: "Houston, we've had a problem here."

When the families and friends at the fire hall are informed of this setback at about 03:00, many of them make a prayer circle asking

---

[156] Our Story, 109

[157] Nine For Nine, 112-113

[158] Miracle at Quecreek, 53

[159] Nine For Nine, 113

[160] Ibid., 113

for God's guidance.[161] Pennsylvania Governor Mark Schweiker asks everyone to pray, then recites Psalm 46: "God is our refuge and strength, always ready to help in times of trouble." He then informs the families of the setback.[162]

Above ground, rescuers start to prepare a second drill site manned by Falcon Drilling from Indiana. Drilling at this site begins at 13:15.[163] Then the site 2 drill also breaks at 150 feet. At that point, the rescuers realize they need to retrieve the broken bit from site 1 so that they can continue drilling. Brandon Fisher from Center Rock Drilling Service calls the manufacturer of drill bit 1 for its' blueprints. With this detail, he designs the overshot specifications for the customized "fishing" unit they need.[164]

Brandon then contacts Star Iron Works in Punxsutawney, Pennsylvania. The owner, Frank Stockdale, informs him that the order will take two and a half days until he finds out what it is needed for and that a National Guard helicopter will transport it as soon as it is completed. He has his workers create the unit in three hours. The helicopter arrives on site at Quecreek just before 16:00. In his second attempt with the "fishing" unit, John Hamilton of Yost Drilling successfully removes the 2,000-pound broken drill bit.[165]

---

[161] Ibid., 117

[162] Ibid., 54

[163] Nine For Nine, 121+124

[164] Miracle at Quecreek Mine, 69

[165] Ibid., 69-70

20:00:

The drilling to reach the miners from site 1 restarts after they insert a twenty-six-inch bit. They are replacing a thirty-inch bit with a twenty-six-inch bit, as they would have had to wait for a thirty-inch to be found and sent. The sixteen-hour delay which the broken bit caused is actually a blessing, as they needed the water level in the mine to be reduced. To Bill Arnold, looking back on the rescue, he sees God's timing and all-knowing power. If the sixteen-hour delay created by the broken bit hadn't occurred, the mine could have decompressed so rapidly that the men would have been killed, crushed by the weight of the water.[166]

Down below: Above all else, the miners want to be out of the blackness.[167]

Saturday, July 27, 2002:

The super drill breaks through to the miners' area at **22:16.** The order is given to shut down all machines on the surface, silencing the compressors feeding air to the men for the first time in three days. John Urosek kneels by the shaft and takes a reading with a pressure gauge, which registers normal atmospheric pressure. They can hear the men below tapping on the drill pipe.

22:53: The rescuers lower a two-way audio device. Bob Zaremski crouches to ground level and begins talking, trying to contact the miners. Miner John Phillippi responds to Zaremski's questions: "Yeah, we can hear you. We're all nine here." Above ground, the

---

[166] Ibid., 71

[167] Nine For Nine, 120

rescue workers are filled with joy, but they keep their feelings low-key until the families can be notified at the fire hall.[168]

Shortly after, police escort John Weir to the fire hall. He waits for the families who were outside to enter, then declares: "We have nine miners, and they are all alive. We're bringing them home."[169]

"The room erupted. In the uproar, and with tears rolling down his cheeks, John Weir thanked God, and then his wife Cindy-...-a pastor shouted, 'Praise the Lord, Praise the Lord!'" The hall resounds with shouts of praise to the Lord. People run outside to celebrate.[170]

At Quecreek number 1 mine, the rescuers celebrate the huge weight that has been lifted off their shoulders. Joe Kostyk and Ron Schad, two of the nine miners who made it to the top on day one, make a prayer circle with some of the other rescuers to give thanks to the Great I AM, the Creator of the universe.[171]

From above, they remove the twenty-six-inch drill that had reached the miners to prepare to replace it with the rescue capsule. Below, the miners have built makeshift walls to protect themselves from the barrage of debris they received until the drill made it to them. The first things that are sent to them are lights, chewing tobacco, and a few snacks. One of the first questions from the miners is if the other team of nine miners has made it. "It was something that had preyed on their minds for the last three days."[172]

---

[168] Ibid., 150, 153-154

[169] Ibid., 155

[170] Ibid., 155-156

[171] Ibid., 158

[172] Ibid., 159-160

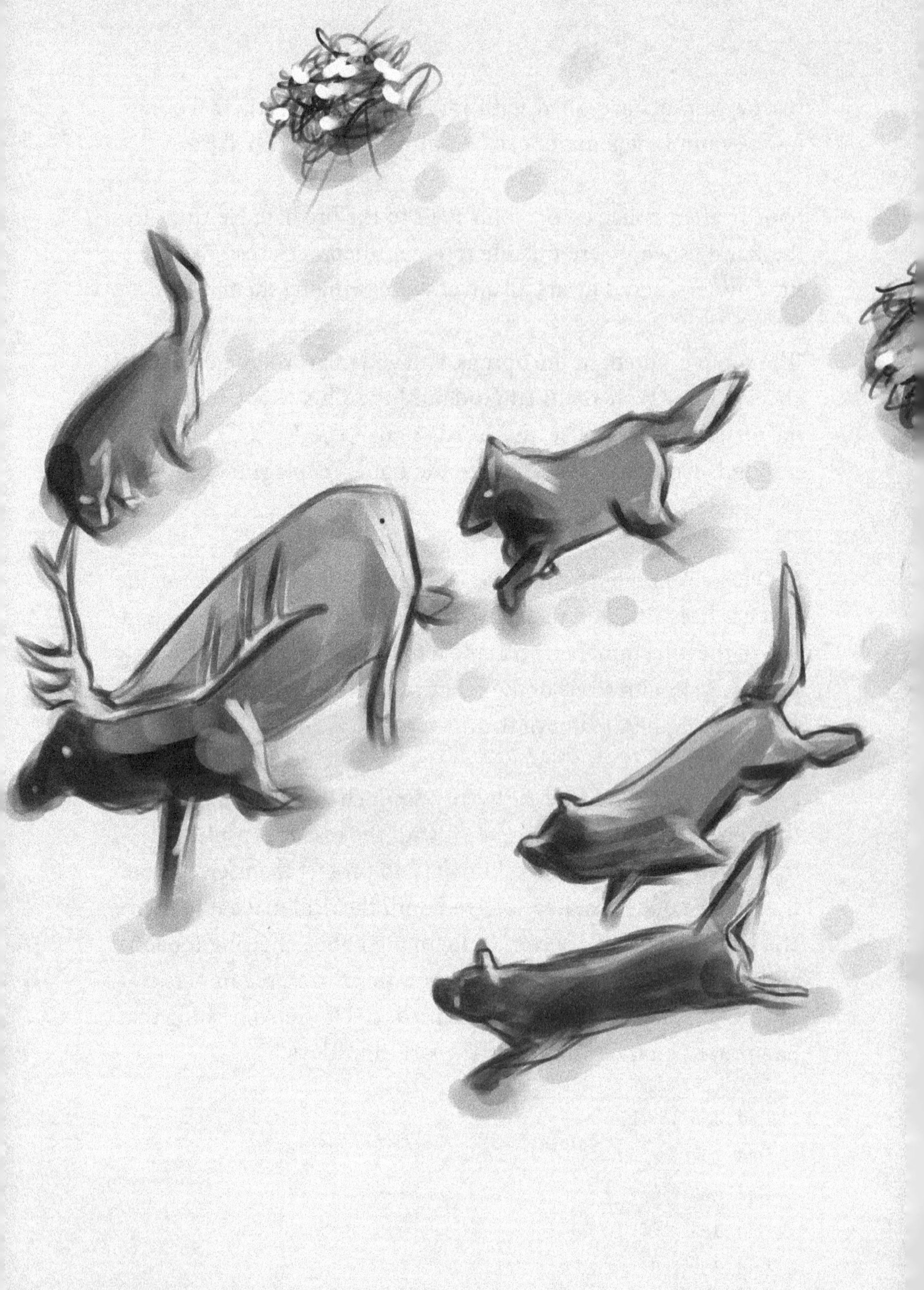

10 The thief cometh not, but for to steal, and to kill, and to destroy: I am come that they might have life, and that they might have it more abundantly.

11 I am the good shepherd: the good shepherd giveth his life for the sheep.

- John 10:10-11 (KJV).

Sunday, July 28, 2002:
12:50:

The first miner, Randy Fogle, is raised to the surface. "As with those to follow, the whites of his eyes shone from a face black with coal dust. They looked like drowned rats-...-the drill shaft had gone through an aquifer, drenching the miners in yet another torrent of cold water in their final exits."[173]

Each man is placed on a stretcher then smoothly delivered to the decontamination unit. The last man out is Mark Poperrnak at **02:45.** He was alone in the mine after the next to the last miner, Robert Pugh, Jr., left in the escape pod. It was the second time he was alone. The first time was when he was separated from his brothers by the raging waters when the breach first occurred Wednesday evening.[174]

After the second miner, Blaine Mayhugh, is brought up, his wife is driven to the hospital where he has been taken to be examined. On the way, they pass groups of people standing and cheering, blowing horns and waving makeshift cardboard signs with the phrase

---

[173] All Nine Alive, 65

[174] Miracle at Quecreek Mine, 80-81

"Nine for Nine." Somerset County is celebrating the triumph of faith and resolve over death and despair. Millions of Americans watching this live on television give thanks for the rescue of the miners' lives.[175]

03:30:

On Sunday, Governor Schweiker gives his last press conference, where he praises the efforts of the rescue workers. "Like the scientists and engineers who brought Apollo 13 back to earth after its space mission went awry, the rescuers were the unsung heroes of this incredible operation."[176] There were about 300 people working on the rescue.[177]

The Aftermath:

There were so many examples of people, companies, and organizations contributing to the rescue. Here are some:

(1) Both engineer Joe Gallo and mine superintendent Dave Rebuck used their extensive contact list to call local drill companies, engineers, and technicians "who would locate the point on the surface that corresponded precisely to the position of the highest point of the mine."[178]

(2) A major issue that had to be dealt with was the amount of material that would be coming out of the rescue shaft. Enormous amounts of ground, limestone, foam, and

---

[175] Nine For Nine, 167
[176] Ibid., 173
[177] Ibid., 161
[178] Ibid., 79

water would be discharged as they drilled a thirty-inch-shaft 240-feet into the earth.[179]

As a result of conversations between Bill Arnold and Larry Neff from Beth Energy Mine, they built a coffer dam: a temporary wall to divert and filter water and debris so that it wouldn't clog the draining. Bill Arnold called a contact at New Enterprise Stone and Lime Company, who supplied about ten truckloads of various sizes of stone. The largest, number-four stone, is the size of a basketball. Bill also called a local farmer, who provided the straw bales they needed for the coffer dam. The goal: to prevent the drainpipe under the highway from being backed up.[180]

(3) In order to use the RD-50 super drill, preparations had to be made. They needed pipe: twenty-feet long, thirty-six inches in diameter, at least 3/8 inches thick. Bill Arnold called Marmon Steel in Pittsburgh, where he had an account, sometime between 2 and 3 a.m. By God's hand, the cleaning lady picked up and relayed the order and its' emergency to the owner, who then called Bill and had the order delivered in less than an hour.[181]

(4) A truck driver was staying overnight in a Somerset hotel before delivering two water pumps with a capacity of 3,000 gallons a minute to Indiana when he heard the news and on his own drove to the site for their use. In a similar case, a pump with a capacity of 7,000 gallons a minute

---

[179] Miracle at Quecreek Mine, 45

[180] Ibid., 46-47

[181] Ibid., 42-43

was headed out of state when the governor of New Jersey redirected it to Quecreek.[182]

(5) Once the drills started on Thursday to pump air to the miners followed by the big super drills to reach the men to bring them to the surface, these machines needed massive amounts of diesel fuel. Bill Arnold's supplier, Agway Fuel, sent a delivery, and then a second fuel company joined, as, for example, the RD-50 super drill required 5,000 to 7,000 gallons every three hours.[183]

(6) A member of the Somerset county's 9-1-1 communications center, Jeremy Coughenoun, remembered that his former Sunday school teacher worked for Sperry Drilling and called her. She drove to the home of her supervisor. By midnight, Sperry Drilling employees and equipment were on site with a drill truck and casing.[184]

(7) John Wier was the spokesman for PBS Coals, the owner of both the area in Shanksville, where Flight 93 crashed September 11th, and the Quecreek Mine. "He was more used to discussing drainage, infill, and reclamation, inhabiting a world of excavations, rigs and pumps-….-He had been the company's spokesman when the hijacked Flight 93 had crashed on PBS land at Shanksville, but nothing had prepared him for this, standing before a roomful of people, seeing the hope in their eyes, the anticipation in their faces."[185]

---

[182] Ibid., 51-52

[183] Ibid., 36-37

[184] Nine For Nine, 79

[185] Ibid., 115

82 | *God's Lessons*

(8) The local restaurants, the Red Cross, and the Salvation Army provided food, blankets, and cots for families and rescue workers.[186]

(9) The seven pastors and the one priest, representing the eight churches the miners attended, provided prayers, encouragement, and guidance for the families and the rescue workers.

(10) All nine miners from the team that made it to the surface on day one stayed on site all four days until their brothers made it to the top: Barry Carlson, Doug Custer, Joe Kostyk, Wendell Horner, Ryan and Dave Petree, Ron Schad, Frank Stewart, and Larry Summerville. "Nine for Nine."

(11) Larry Neff was a consultant for Beth Energy Mine. Initially, Duane Yost had called him Thursday, asking him to set up the pipe Yost needed for his RD-50 super drill. He then stayed on, helping to manage the multiple tasks: "He always knew exactly what was going on. He was thinking at least twenty-four hours ahead of where he was right now. He had four different possible scenarios worked out in his head, and he knew how he would resolve each scenario if it did happen." Many rescue workers assumed he was in charge.[187]

A Governor Schweiker observation: "Looking back, we experienced much more than a successful rescue; we encountered the

---

[186] Miracle at Quecreek Mine, 99

[187] Ibid., 38-39

mighty hand of divine providence guiding us to an outcome that observers now call **the miracle at Quecreek**."[188]

MHSA (The Mine Safety and Health Administration) engineer Gerry Davis: "Our Lord Jesus Christ was the tenth man down there. I give Him the glory. He wrote the script and we were His instruments."[189]

Miner Robert Pugh: "I've never prayed so much in my life. God is the one who got us through this. We all knew we had to rely on God. Faith in God is all that mattered."[190]

TV journalist Wendy Bell on her feelings about the successful rescue on Sunday, after being on live television twenty-four hours straight:

"As I drove that lonely country road back to my family in Pittsburgh, completely exhausted, it all became so perfectly clear. I counted scores of American flags proudly basking in the sun outside farmhouses and businesses and tiny little cottages. Their glorious stars representing faith. The red and white stripes—the glue holding us together.

We Are America. Land of the Free. And for a brief moment in the lush countryside and rolling hills of western Pennsylvania, we were united by a single, common goal: To bring nine men blackened by coal ash and soaked to their cores back up to dry land and into the loving arms of their families."[191]

---

[188] Ibid., 1

[189] Nine For Nine, 173

[190] Ibid., 120

[191] Miracle at Quecreek Mine, 13

Bill Arnold, owner of Dormel Farms, opened his land to be used for the drilling required to pump oxygen to the miners and then to bring them to the surface. He worked from early Thursday morning, when he investigated noises, through to the Sunday rescue. He has established The Quecreek Mine Rescue Memorial and Monument for Life on site to honor both the miners and the rescuers. The address is 140 Haupt Road, Somerset, Pennsylvania.

One of the items on site is a bronze plaque donated by Mathews Bronze company in Pittsburgh. The company had done the same to create plaques for the World Trade Center, the Pentagon, and Flight 93 to remember the September 11th attacks by the Muslim terrorists. What's inscribed are words that Mr. Arnold had written down months after the rescue on a feed sack after he planted nine evergreen trees and a red oak tree on the memorial site to honor the rescue:

> "The symbol of the red oak, here, is of course, faith. The nine evergreens are to represent miners, but in a larger sense, all of us. We all must sometimes bind ourselves together as 'the nine' did when the leaves of faith have fallen like that of the oak in autumn. When we long for the shelter of the oak to protect us from the cold and dark, we must realize that in the coldest winter of our lives, or the darkest mine, when there seems to be no life in the oak—His roots run deep. His limbs outstretched—calling us to Him. And in His shadows, we will all be reborn in spring."[192]

---

[192] Ibid., 97

Another item on site, unveiled in July of 2003, is a seven-foot cast bronze statue made by Alan Cottrill of a miner reading a scripture in the Bible.[193]

Consider visiting both the Quecreek Mine Rescue Memorial and then the Flight 93 site in Shanksville, Pennsylvania, which honors the passengers of that jet which forced the terrorists to crash before their intended target in Washington, D.C., on September 11th.

"Of these two incidents, one celebrates death and valor, the other life and heroism; both are incredible stories of tragedy and triumph. These two shrines, just ten miles apart, now serve as bookends to the human spirit, to man's humanity and inhumanity."[194]

On Sunday, October 4, 2002, a "Community Service of Praise, Prayer, and Thanksgiving" was held at Christ Casebeer Lutheran Church at 7:00 p.m., attended by all eighteen miners and their families. The nine who were rescued via the capsule were: Randy Fogle, Tom Foy, Dennis J. Hall, Ron Hileman, Blaine Mayhugh, John Phillippi, Mark Popernak, Robert Pugh Jr., and John Unger. The hymn "Great Is Thy Faithfulness" was sung, followed by the song "Morning Has Broken" then "O Lord Hear My Prayer," ending with the hymn "Amazing Grace." The scriptures in order were Psalm 23 (The Lord is my Shepherd), Psalm 103 (Praise for the Lord's Mercies), Romans 8:12-25 (Live by the Spirit), and John 1:1-5 (In the beginning was God's Word) and 9-13 (John the Baptist foretold of the coming of Jesus, the light of the world), ending with The Lord's Prayer (Our Father Who Art in Heaven).[195]

---

[193] Ibid., 98-99

[194] Nine For Nine, 192

[195] Ibid., 177

"The reading of Psalm 40, 'I wait patiently for the Lord, he turned to me and heard my cry. He lifted me out of the slimy pit, out of the mud and mire, he set my feet on a rock,' was seen by many as entirely fitting to this epic struggle."[196]

"Future generations need to be able to look at the events that took place here and see Who was in charge. There were hundreds of human hands involved in the rescue, but every one of those volunteers will acknowledge that without divine intervention, the rescue of all nine miners never would have happened-…-find out all the details of what went on, and you will realize the power to what took place. There can be no doubt that this was the work of the Hand of God. It wasn't what we did. It was what He did through us."[197]

Once home, crew foreman Randy Fogle would often get up early to watch the sunrise, appreciating his rebirth.[198]

Brandon Fisher and one of his workers from his company, Center Rock Drilling Service, went to Chile in 2010 to use their super drill in the Chilean Mine rescue, thanks to UPS shipping it free of charge to the remote desert area.

The Quecreek Mine reopened in 2002 and produced coal until 2018. A coal sample taken on the day it closed can be viewed at the Quecreek Mine Rescue museum.

---

[196] Ibid., 177-178

[197] Miracle at Quecreek Mine, 16

[198] All Nine Alive, 75

Peter Walton | 87

BIBLIOGRAPHY

For the Chilean Mine Rescue:

Deep Down Dark: The Untold Story of 33 Men in a Chilean Mine and the Miracle That Set Them Free by Hector Tobar published by Picador Paperback 2014

33 Men: Inside the Miraculous Survival and Dramatic Rescue of the Chilean Miners by Jonathan Franklin published by Berkley Publishing Group 2011

Trapped: How the World Rescued 33 Miners From 2,000 Feet Below the Chilean Desert by Marc Aaronson published by Atheneum Books 2011

Around the Year: A Book of Daily Readings by Emmet Fox. Harper One. Second Edition printed 1992. Emmet Fox lived on earth from 1886–1951.

For the Quecreek Mine Rescue:

Miracle at Quecreek Mine by Bill Arnold published by Encourage Publishing 2017

Nine For Nine: The Pennsylvania Mine Rescue by Andrew Morton 2002 published by Michael O'Mara Books Limited London

Our Story: 77 Hours That Tested Our Friendship And Our Faith. By the Quecreek Miners as told to Jeff Goodell published by Hyperion New York 2002

All Nine Alive Pittsburgh Post-Gazette 2002 Triumph Books Chicago